Happy Ever After

Financial Freedom Isn't a Fairy Tale

The Seven Dollar Millionaire

This edition first published 2021

© 2021 John Wiley & Sons, Ltd

Registered office
John Wiley & Sons Ltd, The Atrium, Southern Gate, Chichester, West Sussex, PO19 8SQ, United Kingdom

For details of our global editorial offices, for customer services and for information about how to apply for permission to reuse the copyright material in this book please see our website at www.wiley.com.

Wiley publishes in a variety of print and electronic formats and by print-on-demand. Some material included with standard print versions of this book may not be included in e-books or in print-on-demand. If this book refers to media such as a CD or DVD that is not included in the version you purchased, you may download this material at http://booksupport. wiley.com. For more information about Wiley products, visit www.wiley. com.

Designations used by companies to distinguish their products are often claimed as trademarks. All brand names and product names used in this book are trade names, service marks, trademarks or registered trademarks of their respective owners. The publisher is not associated with any product or vendor mentioned in this book.

Limit of Liability/Disclaimer of Warranty: While the publisher and author have used their best efforts in preparing this book, they make no representations or warranties with respect to the accuracy or completeness of the contents of this book and specifically disclaim any implied warranties of merchantability or fitness for a particular purpose. It is sold on the understanding that the publisher is not engaged in rendering professional services and neither the publisher nor the author shall be liable for damages arising herefrom. If professional advice or other expert assistance is required, the services of a competent professional should be sought.

Library of Congress Cataloging-in-Publication Data is Available

ISBN 978-1-119-78072-4 (paperback)
ISBN 978-1-119-78074-8 (ePub)
ISBN 978-1-119-78073-1 (ePDF)

Cover Design and Illustration: Jo Sanders and Koh Soo Peng

Set in 10.5/13, ITCGaramondStd by SPi Gobal, Chennai, India

SKY28C33073-C074-4E1B-8929-2C72D2889792_020321

Contents

Acknowledgements

First and foremost, thank you for buying this book, or at least thinking about buying it long enough to read this far. The "Seven Dollar Millionaire" project is not-for-profit, and any money we make doing this will help us reach more people who can't afford to buy books that teach them how to build a more secure future.

The world needs to change, we need to change how, when and how much we teach people about money, and it will need a lot of people picking up a lot of books to create that change.

This book alone has already needed a lot of people. It needed my older daughter Aliya asking me "How much money should I save to become a millionaire?" to come up with the Seven Dollar Millionaire pseudonym we now use for all our projects, reading and editing along the way. It needed my younger daughter Maya to make videos for the Indiegogo campaign that enabled us to launch our first title "The Thousand Dollar Journal." That both of them have now opened savings and investment accounts makes this book a success for my family at least!

It has needed the invaluable support of the organisers, volunteers and students at migrant worker organisations in Singapore, in particular HOME and ASKI Global, to patiently let me teach their existing materials, review them, try out new ideas and provide feedback all the way along, for what worked and what didn't. Thanks also to the international volunteer students at the National University of Singapore who helped test these ideas out, and particularly Dalis Chan for always being ready with an answer or idea.

The illustrations of Jo Sanders and the designs of Soo Peng Koh at Nimbus Design have been vital in transforming the text into something much more visual and engaging. Thank you so much for contributing to this project in ways I couldn't begin to imagine.

Thank you also to the supporters of the Indiegogo campaign that helped us launch The Thousand Dollar Journal, and give away more than 1,000 copies of that journal to migrant workers: Dan Liebau, Jon Foster, Velisarios Kattoulas, Herald van der Linde and The Woke Salaryman chief among them.

Thank you also to the team at Wiley, led by Syd and Purvi, who have guided this along so seamlessly. They have enabled a book that really was initially intended just for my daughter to hopefully reach many more people's daughters, and perhaps even some sons, and for that I am extremely grateful.

And, of course, thanks to my wife, Salina, who patiently believed I was working on a book and not just browsing the internet when glued to my laptop in early mornings and through weekends. Thank you for that, and of course, everything else!

Preface: Once Upon A Time . . .

Everything that follows was originally written as a gift to my daughter as she was planning to leave home and attend university halfway across the world.

When she was little, I promised myself I would write her stories, fairy tales of rainbow unicorns, dragons and adventurous quests, but I never did. I was too busy working to write fairy tales. Lots of nights I was too tired – or just not there – to even read stories to her that other people had written.

I was still busy trying to make money as I wrote this, waking up at dawn to write before work, but I did it to help her learn how to make sure she never becomes too busy with work to pursue her own dreams.

She wasn't the only person I wrote this book for. I also wrote it for students I taught at HOME (Humanitarian Organisation for Migrant Economics) and Aski Global in Singapore.

Every Sunday, migrant workers attend classes organised by these and other charities to learn the basics of budgeting, saving and investing. They have travelled thousands of miles in search of a better life, often coming from tiny villages or remote islands with little evidence of modernity, to the world's most advanced and expensive cities. They risk so much: many are women whose jobs require living with a strange family for years. There are far too many horror stories to recount here, but still they come, risking so much in the hope that they will be able to save enough from their higher income abroad to change their families' lives at home.

I wrote this book, a course based on it and a subsequent saving planner called *The Thousand Dollar Journal* to be a guide for them, a route for them to lift their families out of poverty and support them on their road to financial independence.

At all points in between these two totally different readers – a privately educated university student and migrant domestic workers – we live with a poverty of financial education. This is a poverty of knowledge that creates real-world financial poverty as well as other extreme social problems:

1. Fifty percent of all American households have not saved enough for retirement, according to the National Retirement Risk Index, which recommends saving 15% of your income over your life. The US personal saving rate was 2.4% in 2017, one sixth of that requirement.

2. The UK pension fund Royal London calls this problem the "pension mountain" that future generations will need to scale.

3. And it's not just about retirement . . . 27% of UK respondents to a survey by ING said they had no emergency savings at all. Zero. That's worse than the US (21%) or Australia (22%).

4. Instead, they have debt, in many cases expensive credit card debt: 40% of US respondents, 30% of Australians and 27% in the UK have credit card

debt. Almost half of US respondents said they would struggle if interest rates increase.

5. On top of that, housing markets get ever more expensive, costing 8.5 times the median salary in London, and 12.9 times median salaries in Sydney, according to Demographia (which defines affordable housing as being below 3 times median salaries). If you are saving 10% of your salary towards a house, that's a good start, but it could still take you 129 years in Sydney (if you don't invest).

6. And what advice do young people receive? "Don't eat avocado toast!" Yes, we're going there.

Hardly anyone I speak to knows the two most important formulas in this book, even though they are pretty straightforward:

• That you can become a millionaire by saving just $7 a day and investing it for 7% returns.

• That you can build wealth worth 25 times your spending, and then never need to work again.

I don't blame them: the evidence we see around us suggests that the formulas are wrong, because no one lives this way, even though financial independence should be a universal desire.

Without being told that it is possible, and how to attain it, too many of us believe it is impossible and so don't try for it.

The formulas are right though. First, arithmetic doesn't lie to you.

Second, real people are doing this. An emerging sub-culture of FIRE (Financial Independence Retire Early) enthusiasts are proving it can be done: slashing spending, saving the difference to invest, so they can live well and free years if not decades before their official retirement would otherwise start.

We could and should all know how to do this; but we don't.

More than ever before, this information is becoming critical. Young people face a mountain to climb, in the form of over-inflated property prices and under-inflated wages, and a much lower chance of proper pension provision by their governments than past generations.

They will need the information and skills to be more independent and choose to follow their own path to freedom. They can't be expected to choose a path that they aren't shown and don't know exists, though.

People like the students at HOME want to learn about money, but they have never been taught about it. They desperately want to save and invest, having seen all too closely what poverty does, but as every new dollar of income goes out of the door, they find themselves no nearer to security. Without a plan that has financial security as a clearly defined end-goal, ending their cycle of poverty can seem like just another fairy tale.

I am no different. My own financial education only came about because the job I really wanted – not in finance – fell through, and with a newborn daughter I became a financial analyst by mistake. Many years of working in finance and learning about investing later, it stunned me that the most basic lessons we all need to know about money are never taught to us. The move to near universal literacy has taken 200 years and a huge effort; if we want to eradicate poverty, we need to start making the same efforts about understanding the fundamentals of personal finance.

There are a series of seven stages we all need to go through to achieve financial independence that I call the M.I.S.S.I.O.N. for ease of remembering and to give a sense of its purpose.

Each stage of the M.I.S.S.I.O.N. contains useful information: how to earn more money, how to save more of it and spend less, start investing in and owning assets that could help improve or even save our lives. Put simply: a bit more money in, a bit less out, the difference saved and invested, and financial independence can be yours. Not immediately, but eventually.

You don't have to shoot for the stars or invest like a hedge fund manager. Saving $7 every day and investing it for 7% average returns will turn you into a millionaire over your lifetime. Small changes yield big results.

That's where my pen-name comes from. One day, as I was teaching her the huge impact of compounded returns, my daughter asked me a seemingly simple question: "What's the smallest amount of money I need to save to become a millionaire?" I didn't know, so calculated the answer: $7. A seemingly simple question has a spectacularly impactful answer. Seven dollars of saving and 50 years of investing for 7% returns, and you will be a millionaire. It's within reach of so much of the planet.

The Seven Dollar Millionaire has now become a team of people, including writers, student researchers, designers and illustrators who all want to help people learn how to take control of their lives. In just three words it provides a short-term goal ($7), an aspirational long-term goal ($1,000,000!) and a quick glimpse of the power of compounded returns: it's a three-word financial education, and so we use it as the name for everything we do, of which you can see more at www .sevendollarmillionaire.com.

Although you might think that full financial independence might be impossible, or too far away, knowing that end goal is important. Without it, many of us don't have a good enough reason to know why we are saving and investing, and not just spending everything right now. Pensions and savings can seem dull; but freedom isn't.

It's the freedom enough money provides that can enable you to follow paths and choices that then make you happy. The goal of this book is to help you understand finance enough that you don't have to worry about money. If never worrying about money and being free to follow your best life choices and find fulfillment is your kind of happy then yes, really, *Happy Ever After* starts here.

Introduction: Are You Happy Now?

Are you happy right now? Will you be *Happy Ever After?*

I hope so.

There's really no reason not to be. We live in a breathtakingly beautiful world full of literally every opportunity under the sun, and have a life that we should use to make the most of all those possibilities, doing things we perhaps never even dreamt were possible.

With all of that potential, I hope it doesn't seem too boring to worry about money.

Unfortunately, it's what most of us do. It's the thing that most regularly gets between our happiness and us. Think about it: right now, if you're young and healthy but not doing the one thing you really want to do or chasing your most important goal, the most likely reason is money.

If you don't learn to get money under control, this will be the case for the rest of your life.

It isn't that money makes you happy: it doesn't, can't and won't. That's just a fairy tale. Spending it might bring fleeting enjoyment, but worrying about not having enough money can last years, sometimes destroying lives and families.

Just trying to get enough money can stop us living the life we really want to live.

- Delaying starting that dream project you've always wanted to try because you have to make some cash first.

- Staying late in the office again so the kids are asleep before you get home.

- Another year gone by, with the only highlight a one-week holiday that you will barely remember in a few years, but which cost a year of "savings".

Sadly, that's the best of it – the luxury end of the problem. That's for people who aren't in danger of spiraling into poverty, or desperately trying to climb out of it.

- The 59% of Americans who according to a Bankrate survey in late 2019 said they couldn't scrape together US$1,000 for an emergency – and of course, we all got that emergency in 2020.

- In 2018, the incidence of mental illness in young British people was judged to have increased due to their worries about never being able to afford to own a house.

- Perhaps most shocking of all, in one of the richest and safest countries in the world, old Japanese women are increasingly committing petty crimes, deliberately, to be caught and go to jail, rather than live in poverty outside jail.

Let's not forget the 150 million people on the planet who have left their home countries to find better-paid work, leaving behind families and security to get more money, sometimes taking life-threatening risks to do so.

Yet we can all learn how to build our own financial freedom. Many of us will earn more than enough money in our lives to become millionaires, but we need to know how to do it.

While literacy levels across the world have surged in the last 200 years, from 12% in 1800 to nearer 86% today, financial literacy rates have stood still or possibly even gone backwards. Charles Dickens's line from *Great Expectations* of "Annual income twenty pounds, annual expenditure nineteen pounds nineteen and six, result happiness. Annual income twenty pounds, annual expenditure twenty pounds nought and six, result misery", is quoted as much by the financially literate today as it probably was then, and is as likely to be ignored by the rest of the world as it was then too.

The reality is that while the need for financial security is perhaps greater than it has ever been in the modern era, the tools for financial control of our lives are easier to find than ever before.

We can learn how to be in control of money, rather than money being the thing that controls our life. We can spend less money – and spend much more of our lives being happy. While it might not be the most fun thing in the world, we all need to learn the basics of personal finance, how to earn more, save more and invest more so that more of our lives can be free.

So that we can be *happy*, right now, and hopefully *ever after*.

Stop Believing In Fairy Tales

Most people don't really understand money, so instead they believe in fairy tales. They believe happy positive fairy tales – like they'll win the lottery jackpot or a prince will save them – and they believe negative ones – that achieving independence will never be possible for them, or that investing is just gambling, even if they're told how other people do it.

These are all just myths. They have no substance in reality, but because we aren't taught how money really works, we believe the fairy tales instead.

We might as well be children laying a trail of breadcrumbs in the forest for all the help these stories will do for our finances and our future.

- If we meet the right person, be they prince, princess or pauper, they will take care of our money worries.

- If we buy the magic ticket, in a lottery or the stock market, we will be rich beyond our wildest dreams and never worry again.

- In the magic kingdom we live in, the government will take care of all our needs when we are old or sick.

- We don't need to think or learn about money. We can just spend what we have and everything will work out ok.

There are so many financial fairy tales out there, you could fill a thousand books with them – and still not stop. And yet the truth is so much simpler: if you can understand a few basic rules of personal finance, you can be in control of your own life, working away from debt and towards financial freedom.

And yes, this means you. You might think you have nothing to save, need to keep spending and can't learn to invest, but these are just as much myths as charming princes and talking frogs.

You can do these things. You might not be able to do all of them now, but you can do some of them, and even doing just one of them will build a habit that could grow into the others.

- You can think of one thing you can spend a little less money on. And then you will think of a few more.

- You can find one way to earn a bit more income.

- You can pay some debt down faster.

- Start building an emergency fund that could stop you borrowing the next time you need fast cash . . .

- And you could turn that into the beginning of an investment fund.

- And if you really, really can't do it today, then you can learn how to do it today, so you can do it tomorrow, when your circumstances change.

- Or teach it to your children, so they know how to do this straight out of school and don't make the mistakes you know you made.

You can do at least one of those things. You might have to start very small, but that's how worthwhile things begin and where you can make a real difference, for yourself.

That's the real world – where fantasy ends and reality begins – the things that you can do for yourself. I know that's not magical, but that's the way the world works. There isn't a talking frog who can tell us what we are supposed to do every step of the way.

Or is there?

"This isn't a fairy tale, Princess."

This Isn't A Fairy Tale, Princess!

Once upon a time, in what seemed very much like a magical land, there lived a beautiful princess.

Well . . . what other kind of princess would live in a magical land except a beautiful one? It wouldn't be a spoiled one or one who had never done a day's work in her whole life, would it?

One day, the perhaps-a-little spoiled princess looked out of the window and wondered why all the people were working so incredibly hard, and why they always had been. The farmer was planting his crops and tending his animals. The baker was baking bread and cupcakes. The carpenter was making furniture and helping the builders construct buildings, while market traders were shouting out to passing customers to buy their products.

This had always been the way that things had looked out of her window. People were working, doing their jobs, non-stop. It seemed like the people outside worked hard without ever being able to take a break.

"Working hard ever after doesn't sound that magical," she murmured, half to herself and half to Charlie her pet frog, who strangely always looked like he was listening.

Things inside her father's castle were the same. The cooks were always cooking, the cleaners always cleaning and the guards were always guarding. Even her father, despite being king, still had to do king-type work . . . deals with distant lands, managing the treasury and setting impossible tasks for any visiting prince who came to the castle asking for her hand in marriage.

"Charlie, it seems that the only two people in the castle who don't have to do any work are you and me," she mused to the frog while still gazing out of the window.

"And your days are numbered, princess," croaked Charlie.

"What?" said the princess.

"Yes, I can talk," said Charlie.

"Well, I suppose this is a magical kingdom," the princess mumbled through her shock, although it was what he had said that really worried her. "What do you mean, my days are numbered?"

"This kingdom may be magical," said Charlie, "but there are limits. One day soon, when your education is finished, you're going to have to go out into the world and pay your own way. Nowhere is so magical that people don't have to take care of themselves eventually."

"But what about the prince? The charming handsome one that will finally pass all the impossible challenges my father sets?"

Charlie laughed gutturally, which is the only way a frog can laugh.

"Those princes are idiots," he said, "who have never had to do anything for themselves in their whole lives, which is why your father doesn't want you to marry one. He wants you to be able to take care of yourself first, and then he'll know you'll be free to do whatever you want with your life."

"But . . ."

"But what now?"

"But what about 'they got married and lived happily ever after?'" she pleaded.

Charlie laughed again. "This isn't a fairy tale, princess."

The princess looked at the frog for a long time, as it began to dawn on her that she had a lot to learn.

"And don't even think about kissing me!" said Charlie.

The Chapter I Cheat Sheet

At the start of each stage of the M.I.S.S.I.O.N., we'll give you a quick clue as to what's coming up, so here's one for the whole book:

Aim for the **Freedom Formula,** the calculation of how much money you need to be truly free: when you have assets worth 25 times what you spend in a year, you need never work for money again. You can work for fun, but you won't need to work for money: earn a 7% return on your investment, spend 4%, and the remaining 3% should cover inflation. That's it. You're free to do whatever makes you *Happy Ever After.*

Reaching the **Freedom Formula** requires you to complete a seven-stage M.I.S.S.I.O.N. which is an acronym for the following:

1. **Money.** Money is time and energy. Learn how to think about it properly.

2. **Income.** You need to get money into your life, either by working for other people or working for yourself. The more options you have, the better.

3. **Saving.** Save before you spend and you have a chance of being financially free. Separate your money, and increase saving whenever you can.

4. **Spending.** Learn to enjoy spending more carefully: budgeting, negotiating discounts and reducing careless spending. Cutting back on small things can have a huge impact.

5. **Investing.** The magic of compounding will grow your savings faster all the time, just don't be afraid to take some risk.

6. **Owning.** Understand borrowing, equity and real ownership, to ensure you can achieve your Freedom Formula and financial independence.

7. **Now.** The earlier you start, the more compound interest will work for you, and the less you will have to work. Start now. If you like, you can start here, with these investment service providers: www.sevendollarmillionaire.com/start-here.

CHAPTER 1
The M.I.S.S.I.O.N.

I don't know why we're never taught about money. It's so ever present in our lives that it is almost impossible to explain why no one thinks we need to learn about it.

We get an occasional hint of money in mathematics classes; but at no stage of school are we given a basic grounding in how the world outside really works, what makes it work and, most importantly, how we could make money work for us.

This is huge. Our schools don't teach the one thing we know everyone has to use once they leave school – and because parents aren't taught it, they can't teach it to their own children. As a result, children finish their educations and leave home without ever learning how they will make their way in the world.

Two Facts About Being Free

Compare these two sentences:

1. Most developed countries have a retirement age of between 65 and 70 years old, that is getting older all the time.

2. Many people could stop work comfortably at around half that age, after less than 18 years of working and saving.

Imagine telling people these two facts. Which do you think they will agree with, and which one will get everyone arguing with you?

If you try it (I have), you will find that people will agree with the first statement, because they see evidence for it all around them. But if you tell people they could retire before 40, comfortably independent, able to choose what they do with their lives, you will hear a thousand different arguments and qualifiers.

"Not here, it's too expensive."

"Not with children."

"Not without sacrificing everything I love about my life."

The "fact" that people retire at 70 gets no arguments, because we see evidence for it all around us, even though the evidence is just cultural. It's just what happens. The "retire before 40" argument, while not as anecdotally true, is actually arithmetically true. It's as true as two plus two equals four: it can't be argued with. You can be financially independent even earlier than 35, and you can take some steps that will move you quickly towards freedom at any age.

So let's put those two "facts" into perspective: if you're going to start working at 20, you could work for 50 years, if you only believe what you see around you. Or you could work for less than 18 years, if you believe the numbers. Which do you want to believe?

The M.I.S.S.I.O.N. Stages

The M.I.S.S.I.O.N. can lead you to where you want to be in life. It can enable you to live the life you want to live. It will enable you to have what you want – or help the others you want to help.

The seven stages of the M.I.S.S.I.O.N. can give you the choice to live as you choose, and not as your finances dictate. The M.I.S.S.I.O.N. puts you in control of your money, which puts you in control of your choices, which puts you in control of your life.

Here are those seven stages:

MONEY. It's how we record, store and transfer value. Let's not use that abstract word "value" and instead think of it as things we want and need, like time and energy, and what we do with them. It's how we record, how we give valuable things to other people, or get valuable things from them. And it's how we carry time and energy into the future, so we can have more of them later.

INCOME. This isn't just about getting a job. This is about getting a job that doesn't suck you so dry of enjoyment you feel you need to spend every dollar you earn putting some enjoyment back in your life. It's about understanding that a job is only one way of earning money, and that your own business could be equally as good or better. Think about starting a small side business, and you'll be making extra income, enjoying yourself, making new friends, and learning about business all at the same time.

SAVING comes before Spending. It's true in this book, in this summary; it's true in the dictionary; and it's true for any level of financial success: learn to save before you spend. Even if it's the tiniest amount, it's a habit that has to begin

right away. Start now, and you will be in control
of your life and your future.

Then learn to cut back on SPENDING. You can
have just as much fun cutting back on your
spending as you can actually spending. Spending
is a thoughtless activity, where we just let our
most basic emotions run our lives: cutting back
on spending is a thoughtful and fun game we can
play to win, making us stronger.

INVEST. Once you have enough savings for an emergency fund, you should move your savings into assets
that grow over time. Things like stocks and bonds
and funds that you may not want to understand right
now; and also into things like houses, companies,
movies, cottages in the country, forests with fairies in
them, and other things that sound more fun.

If you OWN this process you can own your own
life. If you do that, you will start to own some
assets, but more importantly, you will have control over your own decisions. Owning your life
means being free and having the potential to be
Happy Ever After.

And the only way you own it is to do it NOW. The
only time to do it is NOW. Start NOW. Continue
NOW. The sooner you start, the sooner the magic
of compound investing will start to work for you.
Yes, there is some magic in this book after all.

And then, one day, much sooner than you think,
you'll be in total control of your life, deciding if you're
going to work solely on the basis of whether you want
to do it, because it excites you and inspires you, not
because you need the money. You'll realise you've
changed your life.

That's freedom.

That's *Happy Ever After*.

The "Freedom Formula"

"Freedom" is the real meaning of *Happy Ever After*: to have the freedom and security and confidence to pursue whatever else you want to do in life.

We all know that money can't buy happiness (even if we don't act like we know it), but it can buy freedom. There's a number that dictates whether you will ever be truly free in your life.

I call it the "Freedom Formula."

Some people call it the "F--- You Number" because it's the amount of money you need to have saved before you can tell your boss to "F---" themselves, but I'm politer than that, just this once (in print!).

Actually, I don't call it that because the Freedom Formula is a little more complicated and a lot more useful. It calculates the exact number you need to be free and it's also a very quick reminder of how to get there (while the M.I.S.S.I.O.N. is a set of detailed directions).

The Freedom Formula is a quick and simple way of telling you how to be free – so simple it contains just two parts ...

Part 1: The Freedom Formula is 25X

You aren't free until you have 25 times your yearly spending in savings and investments. If Jill spends

7

FN10,000 a year, then her Freedom Number is FN250,000. That's it.

I don't often use real currencies like dollars, pounds or yen in this book, because they aren't important and can be distracting. Instead I use "FN" for "Freedom Numbers," or "Fairy Notes." Use the currency of your own real spending to calculate the number you need so it means something to you.

The reason owning assets worth 25 times your spending sets you free is that 4% is a safe rate to take money out of your investments without the real value of those investments shrinking over time: 4% multiplied by 25 is 100%, so if you want to spend 4% of your total assets every year, and you want that to cover all your spending, you need 25 times your annual spending.

That's the Freedom Formula. When your earning assets (not your house if you live in it) equal 25X your spending, you're free.

Part 2: The "X Factor"

I did say there were two parts. The first part is 25, right? Well done, it's 25 times: 25X.

It's not 25 times your salary, though, or 25 times your total income, or anything else like that.

It's 25 times your spending.

That's a crucial difference, because the less you spend on your day-to-day life, the lower your Freedom Formula needs to be. Which puts you in control. It means that saving has a double impact on your Freedom Formula.

> *1.* If you increase your savings, you increase the amount of money going into your investment portfolio, so you get to it faster. That's the easy part of it.

2. Because you can only do two things with money – spend it or save it – more saving equals less spending, which means your "Freedom Formula" decreases – which means you get to it even faster!

The X Factor means that the more you save, the less you spend, the lower your target becomes at the same time as you move towards it faster. It all works together to become easier to achieve.

Remember: Jill was spending FN10,000 a year, with a Freedom Formula of FN250,000. If Jill cut her spending by FN2,000 a year, her Freedom Formula would drop by FN50,000, to FN200,000.

Adding an extra FN2,000 a year to her savings will be good, but it is more important that she cut the amount of savings she needed by FN50,000.

Why The Freedom Formula Is So Important

We're all told we should save, but we don't really know why. For retirement, for a house, for a holiday, for emergencies, for a rainy day, for a poorly defined, hard-to-imagine future that can feel like yet another fairy tale.

We could be saving to be free. We should be saving to be free.

Imagine that instead of working for 50 years or more, from 20 to 70 or even 80 years old, we could be free after less than 18 years. Seventeen and a bit years of admittedly hard work, disciplined saving, reduced spending and clever investing – or 50 to 60 years of less disciplined saving, less clever investing, but lots more hard work.

It will be harder to save that much that quickly, but it might give you the whole rest of your life free.

Think about it: rather than a career of 50 to 60 years, you could work for 18 years, and have the rest of your life to yourself.

You can be doing what you want to do by your mid-30s, and then for the rest of your life, as long as you understand your M.I.S.S.I.O.N. and do what you have to do. That's why it's called *Happy Ever After*.

That should be the goal of saving. That's why it is so important.

And Why Everyone Should Know The Formula

People regularly tell me that the Freedom Formula doesn't apply to everyone.

I hear that said about poor people living in developing countries and I hear it said about rich people living in expensive cities. Poor people tell me that only rich people can do this, and rich people tell me they can't because their lifestyles are so expensive.

(Yes, I know how that sounds!)

I hear so many people say it doesn't apply to them that it would be tempting to believe it doesn't apply to anyone. And yet I know it applies, and can apply, to anyone. Anywhere.

It's important even for those unfortunate people to whom it really doesn't apply, who really would never be able to achieve the Freedom Formula even if they never spent a cent on anything other than absolute essentials.

It's important for them because the steps, learning to save and invest, will be a huge help, even if they are only ever able to save enough for an emergency fund before the next crisis strikes. It will help them avoid taking expensive loans that could force them back into poverty. For them, that could result in far more happiness than the rest of us might feel from an increase in our freedom.

As one older lady at HOME pointed out, it's also important for us to learn so that we can teach our children, so that they can achieve financial independence much earlier than us. And when she said that, it was one of those occasions when the gulf between us closed, because that's why I wrote this book: so that my own daughter could know that this is possible, that it isn't just a fairy tale.

"Out Of The Woods"

Some fairy tales are about princesses and frogs. Lots more are about the scary forest at the edge of the village, the one that children go into and never come out of, the one where the witch lives and the wolf pretends to be your grandmother. It's such a common idea that the phrase "out of the woods" still means getting out of trouble centuries after most of our ancestors moved into the city.

The fact that we no longer live near the woods and have forgotten they are dangerous doesn't mean we know how to get out of today's woods. It means we don't even know we're in them.

We could be lost in the woods our whole lives – working in jobs just to stay in the woods, paying off debts for things we didn't really need, never building any real savings or freedom – unless we find the path.

Imagine there's a big scary forest that starts just at the end of our childhood, when we first go to work, and stretches all the way to whenever it is we can't work anymore ...

We may never get out of those woods.

That's most of our lives, in the dark, scary forest, not knowing where we're really going. We step in around 20 years old and spend the rest of our lives in the dark, stumbling, looking for a way out. Or just hoping for a way out, not really knowing how to look for it.

Only at the very beginning and the very end of our lives are we free to choose what we want to do without money being the main concern. Only at the very beginning and the end are we out of the woods.

If we knew a way out of these woods, I am sure we would all definitely use it.

This second forest looks much better, covering only a short period of our lives, maybe as little as 15 to 20 years. After that, once we're out of the woods, we can see where we're going, we can choose our own path. It might not be all sunshine, flowers and butterflies, but it's better than the forest.

If we follow the M.I.S.S.I.O.N. closely, we could be out of the woods in just 18 years.

If you're a good artist, like Jo who drew all the illustrations in this book, you could draw yourself a version of these woods, to show you when you're going to get out. If you're not, you could draw a simple line like this.

I call it a "life-line." On it, we can draw how many years we would ideally like to work, when we start and when we finish. That can become our target, our way out of the woods.

The Fastest Way Out Of The Woods

If you like the woods, by all means stay there. It's easy. Spend everything you ever earn, and you'll never be out of the woods.

If you save nothing every year, that is where you'll stay. As the chart below shows, saving 0% of your income means working for 100 years, or forever, if that's how long you live.

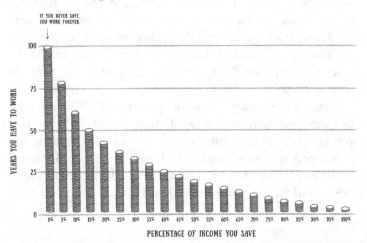

Just a little bit of saving can have a big impact, though. Saving 5% of your income can mean working for 78 years: start at 21 and you'll stop at 99! Saving 10% cuts that back to 60 years, 18 years gained for 5% extra savings!

That's the kind of rate that governments recommend, but they don't care if you enjoy yourself. They may want you to work forever and pay them more tax, after all.

Saving 25% of your income will cut those years of work back from 60 to 35 years, and you can be free in your 50s, which to this 50-year-old is beginning to sound a bit more like it!

But let's take a look at the other end of the scale.

Saving 100% of your income means you're already free, because you don't need to spend any of the money you earn, so you don't really need to earn it.

A slightly more realistic goal of saving 75% of income would set you free in a pretty amazing 8 years. That sounds impossible, but there are people who do this, and they're not billionaires (google Joe and Ali Olson, two teachers who retired after 8 years!).

A more achievable goal of saving 50% of your income will set you free in 17 to 18 years.

If you're young right now, perhaps the idea of saving for the next 78 years doesn't seem all that different from saving for the next 60 or even the next 35. They're all so far into the future as to be never.

But in 17 and a bit years' time, you might be able to stop working entirely if you save 50% of your income.

And in 8 years' time, if you saved 75% of your income and invested it well, that could be you too, sitting in a beach cabana not a cubicle. Putting on plays and not work suits. Helping poor people not a faceless corporation. Growing flowers or great memories, whichever you prefer. Just by giving up on some meaningless spending, you could feel like you haven't missed out on anything in your life.

Try it out for yourself.

Here's another blank life-line: draw on it how much of your life you want to work, and leave blank how much you would like to be free.

Come back to this later in the book, to remember how much you need to change and what you need to learn.

Your M.I.S.S.I.O.N.

Make the M.I.S.S.I.O.N. your own by creating your own plan.

Think about how far you are from your Freedom Formula of 25X your yearly spending. Think about how long you want to take to get there. Work out how much extra you can earn, how much more you can save, how little you can spend and how much better you can invest.

Write these things down right now:

• How long you want to work.

• How much extra you can earn.

• How much extra you can save.

• Where you can cut the most spending.

While the most important, ultimate goal of the M.I.S.S.I.O.N. is financial freedom – having 25X your spending – you can also decide on really important and valuable near-term and medium-term goals. The best 3 are building an emergency fund, creating an investment portfolio and owning some property.

Write these down too:

I will build an emergency fund by this date:

I will start an investment fund by this date:

I will buy my first property by this date:

I will get to the Freedom Formula by this date:

Write down these goals, remember them, and use the rest of this book to create a precise plan for achieving them.

It doesn't matter if you don't achieve them exactly as planned. Having the goals gives you a chance of achieving them that not having them doesn't, so give yourself a chance now and write them down.

Back In The Real World: Money-talk

Try answering a financial literacy quiz, for example the one at finra.org.

Up to 140,000 people around the world have tried answering similar survey questions, and only around a third of them get 3 or more right. If you got more than 3, well done. You're in the top 33% of the planet!

Learning these basic concepts is an important step, because financial literacy is an important step towards independence. Knowing how to calculate annual percentage returns, knowing something about reducing risk and the effects of inflation will all help you understand your finances better.

Learning financial literacy can be dull though. Instead, through this book, we will learn how to become financially free – because that's what we really want – and we'll become financially literate on our way there.

"He's naked again?" the princess asked.

The Emperor's New Money

"Did your father ever tell you about the country on the other side of the magic mountains, where the emperor was really vain and greedy?" Charlie asked the princess.

"Oh, is he the one that walked around his city naked because some tricksters convinced him that he was wearing the most amazing clothes ever?" the princess checked.

"Yes, that one," Charlie croaked. "Thanks for ruining my story."

"Oh sorry, it's a good one. Daddy laughed and laughed and laughed when he heard about it!"

"Well, the Emperor learned his lesson, and used the same trick that was played on him, except no one noticed," Charlie explained.

"He got naked again?" the princess asked.

Charlie then explained how the emperor across the mountains had run back to his palace covered only in embarrassment after his infamous naked walk – and refused to come out for a very long time. While he was hiding, he thought over and over about that day, and one thing seemed stranger than any of the others: not just that he had been taken in by the tricksters, but that everyone else had been fooled by them too. Everyone could see he was naked, but no one had said anything until the little girl shouted out.

"Why was that?" the princess asked.

"Because no one ever really knows what everyone else is thinking," Charlie answered. "So even if one person thinks something is odd, if they see everyone else going along with it, that person normally follows along too. They won't say anything in case it will make them look stupid, instead of the naked guy!"

"That's just silly," said the princess.

"It is," Charlie agreed. "The emperor thought it was silly too, so he decided to test his theory to see if he could get people to do it again, and this time play a huge trick on all the people who had laughed at him on that day."

"What did he do?" the princess asked, thinking it would have to be a really good, really funny prank if it was going to make up for walking around town naked.

"He bought a printing press and printed thousands of little notes with his picture on," Charlie explained.

"What?" asked the princess. "Who would want lots of pictures of the emperor? Did he keep his clothes on in the pictures at least?"

"I don't know," Charlie thought, "it just showed his face, but anyway he told everyone in the empire that they must now start using these pictures of him on paper as money ..."

"Instead of magic gold coins?" interrupted the princess.

"Yes, instead of magic gold coins, and he told the people they had to pay their taxes with these pieces of paper."

"Did the people all laugh at him for being stupid again?" the princess asked.

"No, they didn't. No one laughs about tax," Charlie explained. "People started to pay for the notes with their livestock and produce, and some of them with gold coins they had saved, until the emperor had collected nearly all the magic gold coins in his empire, and everyone was using his worthless pieces of paper instead."

"That's crazy. Did a little girl shout out that they were only paper?"

"Maybe, but no one listened. Life went on just as before, only now the emperor was richer and everyone else was poorer."

"Why were they poorer?" asked the princess.

"Well," said Charlie. "All they had collected was pieces of paper and not magic gold, so the emperor could print a new batch whenever he wanted, making it worth less, and everyone would have to believe him. Second, everyone felt that the paper wasn't as valuable as something real, so although they worked just as hard to get it, they didn't think as carefully before they spent it. All they had were silly little pictures of the emperor in their pockets, so it didn't matter if they spent them on other silly things. No one ever wanted to save them, and so they all became poorer."

"That's terrible," said the princess. "Those poor people. Is there anything we can do?"

"No. No one will believe you if you shout that out in the crowd now," Charlie told her. "All you can do is make sure it doesn't happen to you, and slowly tell everyone you know about it, make sure they understand what money really is and how important it is to be free."

"Ok, what do I need to do ...?"

The Chapter 2 Cheat Sheet

Money

Learning what money really is, if it's not magic gold coins.

1. The first thing money enables us to do is exchange our time and energy for someone else's time and energy.

2. But it also lets us take the value of that time and energy through time, to change it for time and energy at a later date.

3. That's important, because when you're young you have time and energy, but no money.

4. When you're working you have money and energy, but no time.

5. And when you're old, you have no energy, but you do have time and money – if you're lucky!

6. If you save and invest well, you can have money, time and energy before you get too old to enjoy them.

7. It's important to learn what things really cost – in terms of your life.

CHAPTER 2
M for Money

"The price of anything is the amount of life you are prepared to exchange for it."

Henry David Thoreau

If you want to be free of the choices needing money could force you to make, you need to start by knowing what money is.

That may sound easy. We all think we know what money is. We are all so used to money being around us, and it being so important to our lives, that we don't think about it. Instead, we have feelings and emotions about it that aren't rational.

If we've never had money, or even just periods where we didn't have enough, it may have become associated with various emotions. We may think about it too much. We may try to use it to buy happiness or love (which it can't: the old songs weren't wrong).

Even if it's always been easy to get – lucky you – you may fail to respect it properly. You might think that it's not a thing that needs respect, but what you're failing to respect is your own attitude towards it, and its importance in shaping the rest of your life.

Those attitudes don't help our understanding – and won't help us take control of our lives – so let's start by really understanding money.

What is money?

Money is a way of representing, transferring and storing things that are valuable to us, things like time, energy, intelligence or creativity.

- Representing means putting a number on time, energy and creativity so we know how much we value the things that went into getting the money, or the things we want to receive for our money.

- Transfer means how we take our time and energy and exchange them with others.

- Store ... well, it's how money becomes a time machine, enabling us to take things we value into the future for us to use there.

"There are time machines that can take us into the future?" the princess asked Charlie the talking frog.

"Not really," he croaked. "That's science fiction not fairy tales: not my genre. What we can do is take value we create today into the future, so we can use it then."

"That sounds more like Tupperware than a time-machine," the princess pointed out.

"Yes," admitted Charlie. "But Tupperware is still a pretty useful thing."

How do we know any of this is true? The best way is to think about the reasons you let other people have some of your money.

Let's imagine you buy a coffee. Someone put energy and time into growing the beans, intelligence into making the espresso machine, their creativity into designing the cafe, their time brewing the coffee, taking your order and drawing a cartoon frog in the foam. You bought all of these people's time, intelligence, energy and creativity with your money.

Could you do all or any of these things without these other people? Imagine trying …. Well you definitely can't grow your own coffee, unless you're in the right part of the world and possess the right skills. You don't necessarily need the expensive coffee grinding and making machine: you could of course buy instant coffee at the supermarket, although you'll still need a kettle, unless you're planning on starting a fire!

But what if you want to meet someone for a cup of coffee in a nicer environment? Well, you could make some coffee, put it in a thermos flask, and share it with them in the park; but you'll need to buy the thermos. You're going to need money to do any of these things.

Because of money, someone can give you their time and energy, and you can give them yours.

Thoreau put it much better: "the price of anything is the amount of life you are prepared to exchange for it". We're not exchanging money. We're exchanging our time and energy: an "amount of life."

This is how our economy works, and probably always will. It's how we all work in it and why we all work in it.

Money makes things more efficient. It makes our lives better, otherwise we would have to do everything we're bad at, without being able to get anyone to help. No accountants. No cleaners. No pubs, bars or restaurants. No doctors or nurses.

We want money because we want things. We want things from other people who have put their time and energy into those things. Importantly, those people are probably better at making the things we want than we are, so we're happy to pay them.

We're happy about it because there's a beneficial time and energy exchange: it would take us more time and energy for us to make the thing they've made to the same standard, than it would for us to make whatever it is we made with our time and energy that we were able to turn into money and transact with them.

But we also want money not just because it helps us transact the product of our time and energy for other people's time and energy. We want it because it's a good store of our time and energy too.

The Real Cost Of Your Coffee Habit

Before we go back to what money is, let's quickly jump forward to the main point, which is taking control of our lives. It's hard to know how to take control of your life if you don't know what your options are, and how much what you do is actually costing you.

Not in money, because we already know that: if a coffee costs FN5, it costs FN5. That's too easy.

What does it cost in Thoreau's terms? How much life are we giving up to get that coffee? We can look at it in a few different ways:

1. The way most people look at it is to think that it costs part of our total income. Let's imagine we're paid FN24,000 a year, that's FN2,000 a month, and if that month is February, FN100 a working weekday. The FN5 coffee has cost us 5% of one day, so 5% of an 8-hour

workday is 24 minutes. It costs 24 minutes of our working life to buy a coffee. If we take half an hour to sit and drink it, that's not so bad. Let's get one. My treat!

2. We have to spend money on other stuff before we can buy coffee, though. Let's imagine that tax, rent, utilities, basic food and other essentials take up two thirds of our spending. Now we don't get FN100 a day to spend just on stuff we want, we only get FN33. The coffee still costs FN5 though, so now it costs FN5/FN33 multiplied by the hours we work to buy a coffee ... that's 1 hour and 13 minutes. That's longer than it will take to drink, but still not the end of the world. We can still meet for an occasional coffee at that price, but we should probably split the bill.

3. As we're trying to achieve the Freedom Formula, we need to look at the impact coffee has on our saving and freedom. If we save just 5% of our income, or FN5 a day, then a FN5 coffee is now costing us an entire day of saving. Seriously! I want a pretty impressive picture drawn in my foam if I have to work a whole day to get it!

4. If we only save 5% of our income, and invest it for a long-term return of 7%, it will take around 78 years for us to achieve our Freedom Formula. Starting at 20 years old, we will be 98 years old before we're free. If we double the rate at which we save, from 5% of our salary to 10%, which we can do if we don't buy that coffee, it will take us 60 years. We just bought 18 years of freedom with a daily coffee. That's what it's really costing us.

In the past, some writers have over-simplified this and tried to make the numbers look as though you can retire by 40 just by not drinking a latte every now and then. Or buy an expensive house by not eating avocado toast.

Obviously, that's not true, but it should also be just as obvious that spending on things we don't need has an impact. It's not just about kicking the coffee habit, it's about stopping wasteful consumerism and starting changes that can really impact our lives.

In five years, although we won't have bought a house from our coffee savings, we might have saved up an emergency fund worth six months of our spending. That kind of fund is the first step on the path to financial security.

The Cupcake Economy

Money helps us represent and transfer time, energy, creativity and other aspects of our life – but it's better than other things that could do that, because it also stores it efficiently.

Oil, flour and sugar are all stores of energy, for example, but they will go stale after a while. If we take our own energy, we can turn them into cupcakes that will taste amazing; but they will go stale even faster. Whoever else we want things from in life, we will need to get our cupcakes to them at their best. When they're fresh from the oven, our cupcakes will be delicious, and probably worth a lot more than the time and energy we put into them, so we did a good thing baking them.

But then, really quickly, they deteriorate. When they cool down, they're not as nice as when they're hot from the oven; and the next day they're ok, if a little dry.

Then a couple of days later, they're actually just inedible. If that's where we stored our time and energy, then we're not going to get a lot in return. The people who are going to give us their time and energy aren't going to want to. Our time and energy will have disappeared, vanished into nothing. While they would have been worth much more than the combination of ingredients and your time and energy to start with, now they're worth a lot less.

Money is a better, more storable form of time and energy than cupcakes because it doesn't go off. This is really useful, because most of the things we make or do for money are not as storable as money – even over a short period of time.

If we can sell our cupcakes while they're fresh from the oven, we can get more than the value of all the inputs that went into them – sugar, flour, heat, effort – and convert that into money which we can keep for as long as we want.

If money didn't exist, everything would have to take place in the present, and time and energy would not be stored longer than the life of the immediate product. Money enables us to sell our products, our time and our energy from one day, and keep that time and energy to another day. Or month. Or year. It enables time and energy to be carried into the future.

Storing time and energy now will give us time and energy in the future.

As we'll see when we discuss "I for Investing," we can invest the money in assets that can increase in value, that we can then potentially exchange for more time and energy than we put in. If we store money in the right way, we can take out much more than we put in.

The Money Time Machine

We can't predict very much about the future, and even if we don't need a lot of money right now and we are making enough to cover our needs, we don't know that will always be true. We might fall ill and not be able to work. We may have children that need things (toys, education, cupcakes). We may just want to tell our boss to get lost and walk out the door and never work again.

This is one of the truly great things about money. It's like a time machine (or Tupperware). Money can help us take our time, our energy, our creativity and intelligence and give it to ourselves in the future.

We can store it up so that we don't have to use our own energy in the future to get what we need – because we might not be able to make it then. There's a great saying that makes this really memorable:

Time (and Energy) = Money

When we're young, we have time and energy, but no money.
When we're working, we have energy and money, but no time.
When we're old, we have ... no energy.

Ok. I just changed the original version of that saying ... you can probably guess how, but I'll tell you why later.

Young people have all the time and energy

If you've ever wondered why old people love to criticise young people, it's because they're jealous of all the time and energy they have!

We all remember being young and having time and energy but no money. When we're really young, none of us really care about having money. All we need is a sunny day and friends. Maybe a stick or a ball and a patch of ground. We can invent things all day, create whole worlds and new games, and have non-stop fun.

We could pretend we had money, if we needed to, but generally we didn't because we could also pretend that we had anything we wanted, and pretending was as much fun as having the things, if not more.

When you have time and energy – as well as creativity, innocence and a boundless sense of fun – there's not much need for money.

Working people have money but no time

As we get older, our fun becomes a little more expensive, whether that's toys, or sweets, or games, or sports gear. We start to feel that we don't have all the money we need, but we still have plenty of time and energy.

That pressure of not having enough money eventually turns into work. We need to buy food to eat, a place to live and a social life with friends.

In the 1940s, a psychologist called Abraham Maslow proposed that all human needs can be placed on a pyramid in order of fundamental importance, from food and shelter, to status items and higher concerns. When you're in school, that's just a theory, but when you leave school, and have to pay for your own food and shelter, it becomes much more realistic, because no one else is paying any more – and you need food and a place to live.

Soon the other items on Maslow's pyramid become important, such as status items, to show that we aren't just feeding ourselves but that we have relevance and status in the world.

There quickly seem to be more reasons for us to spend money than reasons not to work, and so we earn and spend, earn and spend. Sometimes it can seem that the harder we work and the more we earn, the less time we have money to spend, so we spend it as quickly as we can. It is almost as if the important thing about expensive things is that they are expensive, so you have no money left.

I know that seems totally insane, but look at how people who work just to earn a lot of money actually spend it, and you'll see that they have convinced themselves that cheap things are not worth buying, and only expensive things can deliver the satisfaction they need. The more money you have and the less time, the more money you must spend in that time.

Old people, of course, have no energy

The popular version of this saying is "Old people have time and money, but no energy". It makes the three sentences nicely circular, but sadly it is only rarely true.

A lot of old people have no money at all. They didn't save enough; perhaps because they believed the wrong fairy tale or they thought their children or the government would take care of them, and it didn't happen.

A lot of old people have no money and have to carry on working, so they don't have time either, and the work is really painful, because the one thing we all agree on is they don't have any energy. They then don't have time to enjoy themselves, because they didn't store it up when they were younger. They don't have energy to enjoy themselves, because they didn't store that up when they were younger either. That's what money could have been for them: stored up time and energy.

Admittedly, that's the worst-case scenario, but the original saying "Old people have time and money, but no energy" is hardly the best outcome either. It's actually pretty miserable, if the best you're hoping for is to stop exchanging your time and energy for money at precisely the moment you have no energy left. It's almost as though you're only saving for your retirement care.

The Energy Equation Following The M.I.S.S.I.O.N.

If you complete your M.I.S.S.I.O.N., it should look like this:

> *Young people have time and energy, but no money.*
> *Working people have energy and money, but no time.*
> *The Freedom Formula means you have money, time and energy, Happy Ever After.*

While you're working, converting your time and energy and creativity into money, you can store enough of it for the future to afford to live your life in the way you want to live it, while you still have the energy to enjoy it. The more you store, the better you store it, the sooner that future begins.

It's why money can help us have a good life, if we take control of it.

Your First Step Out Of The Woods

In the old fairy tales about children going into the woods, they had no idea how to get out again. If they strayed too far from the path they would be lost forever.

If you live in a country where you can't rely on anyone to take care of you, and no one ever explains about the importance of money to you, you're worse off than those children, because you don't even know what the path looks like. You could be lost in the woods for the rest of your days.

Even if you save 5 to 10% of your income, you would only be able to retire by the time you're 80, which isn't much to look forward to.

That's not true for you anymore. You've read this far. You've understood that you've got to save at least something for a rainy day, for an emergency, or for your old age.

You know you need to save some money, at least 15% of your income. That way, you will be independent by the age of 70, or after 50 years of working and saving. It might not look like much, but it's a start, and your route out of the woods is already getting shorter.

Are You Ready To Be *Happy Ever After*?

Answer the following questions to see if you can now tell what is true, and what was a fairy tale.

1. **Complete the sentences by filling in the missing words:**

   Young people have time and energy but no _____.

   Working people have energy and _____ but no time.

   Old people have _____ and _____ but no _____.

   Being Happy Ever After means having enough _____, _____ and _____.

2. **When does "saving" come before "spending"?**

   a) In this book.

   b) In any sensible saving plan.

   c) In the dictionary.

   d) In all of the above.

3. **If you earn FN50 every day, and you can find a way to save FN5, what is your saving rate?**

   a) 5%.

   b) 10%.

   c) 0%.

4. **If you can safely live on 4% of your total savings, how many times your annual spending do you need to have saved?**

   a) 40X.

   b) 3X.

   c) 25X.

5. If you spend FN10,000 a year, what is your Freedom Formula?

a) FN100,000.

b) FN250,000.

c) One Million Dollars!!!

d) (A hint: your Freedom Number is 25...)

6. Tick the ways increasing your saving speeds up becoming free:

a) Your savings increase faster.

b) You can build a bigger investment portfolio.

c) Your spending reduces, so your Freedom Number comes down.

d) You will have no friends, so won't need to buy them things.

7. "The price of anything is the amount of ____ you are prepared to exchange for it." What's the missing word?

Answers...

1. Young people have time and energy but no MONEY. Working people have energy and MONEY but no time.
   Old people have MONEY and TIME but no ENERGY.
   Being Happy Ever After means having enough ENERGY, TIME and MONEY.

2. d) All of the above.

3. b) FN5/FN50 is 10%, so that's a 10% saving rate.

4. c) 4% × 25 is 100%, so you need 25X your annual spending.

5. b) 25 × FN10,000 is FN250,000.

6. a, b and c are all correct. Of course you'll still have friends!

7. Life.

Free Money Stuff – *Mr Money Mustache*

One of the best places to continue learning and thinking about money is Mr Money Mustache, who can be found at www.mrmoneymustache.com.

He writes with consistent "bad-assity" (a word I'm not sure whether I'll have to pay him royalties to use) on subjects such as "Luxury Is Just Another Weakness" and "Curing Your Clown-Like Car Habit."

Yes, he gets it.

This is someone we can all learn from. Even if you never want a mustache, you want his attitude to money.

"You shall get a side-gig."

The Cinderella Side-Gig

The puzzled princess still didn't understand. "What about Cinderella?" she begged. "Are you telling me that's not true? That could happen to me too!"

"Hahaha!" croaked the frog for so long that the princess almost started to worry that he couldn't talk anymore, and it was all just a bad dream.

"When was the last time you had to spend the night cleaning the kitchen and then sleep on the cold stone floors?" Charlie asked, when he could finally stop croaking. "You don't even have a stepmother, let alone a wicked one."

"But ..." she begged, "the prince ..."

"... was an idiot, like most princes, doing nothing but holding parties, sending scouts out looking for the prettiest girls in the land, and in the process bankrupting his father," explained Charlie.

"And the glass slipper?"

"One of the prince's stupidest ideas," said Charlie. "They didn't really fit anyone and shattered if you walked on them – a disaster! Let me tell you about the Cinderella I knew ..."

To start with, the princess thought the story sounded roughly the same. Cinderella's mother had died, her father remarried, and she was treated like a servant by her stepmother and stepsisters. It all sounded so terrible that the princess felt the need to interrupt.

"And then the fairy godmother…" she suggested.

"And then Cinderella's real godmother stopped by." explained Charlie. *"She was an old friend of Cinderella's mother, and she saw how much work Cinderella was doing and how well she did her work. She told Cinderella that she shouldn't just do this work for free, and that she could come and live with her, and work as a professional house-cleaner."*

"What? This isn't right!"

"Cinderella's godmother was an independent businesswoman …"

"What did she do?" the princess interrupted Charlie.

"She had a carriage rental business. No, not ones made from pumpkins, princess," Charlie knew he needed to explain, but left out that the carriages needed to be returned before midnight to avoid late charges. *"She told Cinderella that independence was the most important thing in the world, and there was no point hoping a prince would rescue her because, one, princes don't do that – why would they? – and two, that's just swapping dependence on one person for dependence on another.*

"Cinderella's problem wasn't that she was working, it was that she wasn't working to be free."

"So, she ran away to live with her godmother?"

"To start with, yes. Her godmother encouraged her to build a side-business, doing emergency cleaning, called "Cinderella's Magic Helpers." She eventually turned that into her main business, hiring other young ladies who worked too hard for not enough money, helping them make better incomes and provide amazing service. She learnt to save the money she made from that, and invested it wisely so that it could make money all on its own without her doing any work at all. That's how she learnt to take ownership of her life so that she could be free to live any kind of life she wanted, without

relying on a prince, or anyone else, and," concluded Charlie, *"she learnt that she had to do it all right now."*

"Then," corrected the princess. *"She had to do it then."*

"Now, princess. There is no other time," Charlie replied.

"That's a really unsubtle hint that I have to start learning this now too, isn't it?" asked the princess.

"Well, unless you can think of a good reason to delay being 'Happy Ever After'."

After a bit of thought, the princess asked *"Do I have a godmother, fairy or real, who can teach me all of this?"* as she knew that Charlie was right, and she had a lot to learn.

"No," croaked Charlie. *"You have a talking pet frog. I think that's enough make-believe for one story, don't you?"*

The Chapter 3 Cheat Sheet

How We Learn To Make More Money

1. We need to earn some money – income – before we can save it.

2. Rather than just work for someone else who pays us and doesn't care if we enjoy it, we should all explore working for ourselves.

3. Working for yourself means you can keep all the benefit you create, and don't have to share it with your managers and bosses.

4. It also means you create your own job. Imagine how much more likely it is that you create your own dream job, rather than hoping someone else does that for you.

5. "Don't give up your day job." You don't have to. Side-businesses (or side-gigs or side-hustles) are increasingly popular ways of earning extra income, reducing spending and expanding horizons.

6. Side-jobs might help you save more money than the extra you earn, as they could take up time you previously spent socialising or shopping.

7. They could eventually become your main gig!

CHAPTER 3
I For Income

So we know what money is, and we know why we want it. Now we need to know how to get it.

The best way to get money is passively, that's when money works for you, and you don't work for it. It's great; but we need to make some money first, so we can save it and invest it, which is how we make money passively.

To do that, we have to make some money actively ....

How To Make Active Income

All the billions of people in the world make money in just two ways.

- They work for other people, doing what they're told to do.

- Or they work for themselves, doing what they think they should do.

Dream job? Dream on!

Let's get another fairy tale out of the way first: very few people get their dream job. In employee engagement surveys that the Gallup organisation runs across the world, only 15% of respondents say they like theirs. That's not their dream job, either – they just said they liked them.

The rest of us, five out of six, fall into jobs by accident, looking for something to make us money and pay the bills. We aren't taught to do that, but that's what happens.

School teaches us a few skills that might be useful for either our own business or someone else's, but we are then left to work out what we should do on our own. What people do when left on their own is to copy what they see around them, and for most of us, that's people with jobs: parents with jobs, teachers with jobs, friends with jobs and money.

Not businesses.

Businesses look complicated, like there are lots of other things to do in them, not just show up at work and get paid. They look like they need capital and experience, two things most of us don't have when we're young. Most of us haven't been taught to set up a company, or understand its accounts, or manage its marketing budget, or any of the hundreds of things that we imagine we might need to know how to do if we wanted to create our own job.

They look risky, like things do when we don't know much about them and we've heard of people failing at them.

And all of this is true.

So when we want or need money, we normally want or need it quickly, and we don't have time to go to business school and learn those things; so we get a job and hope for the best. We fall into a job and that's our future started.

If we're lucky, we like the job a lot, have a great boss, and do it forever – happy to be paid for doing something we enjoy. Maybe that's the 15% of people who do like their jobs.

More often than not, though, we don't like the job that much.

So we change jobs. And change jobs again. We change and change until we find one that is acceptable. Not inspiring, but acceptable. Or until we can't face changing jobs any more.

Will we have saved enough money by then to do what we really want to do? Probably not.

Instead, we'll have started spending the money we earned to make ourselves feel better. We'll have told ourselves to buy something that's expensive, that we're not entirely sure we want, but we tell ourselves "I earned it." We don't really want that particular thing, but what we do want is the pleasure of doing something we want to do after the displeasure of having spent the day, the week or even the whole year doing something we didn't want to do.

Maybe one of the reasons we're all so addicted to consumerism, spending money on things we don't really want, is because we're so unhappy at work, doing things we don't want to do, that we feel the need to spend on things we impulsively feel we want.

And so we're quickly back where we started ... needing money, and having to work for someone else to get it, doing something we don't want to do, making ourselves unhappy, and then spending money again as we try to chase a little easy happiness.

Some people spend a year of savings on a week's holiday. Some people spend 4 or 5 years of savings on a car they drive for a few hours a week.

Nearly all of us spend more than we should on things we don't need, and things we only want when we want them – and then wish we hadn't bought.

It is the sad cycle of so many people's lives: philosopher Alan Watts probably said it best:

"You'll be doing things you don't like doing in order to go on living, that is, to go on doing things you don't like doing, which is stupid."

You don't often get a philosopher finishing a sentence with "which is stupid," but Alan Watts was talking about something so big, so obvious, and so common across the whole world, that it needed some straightforward language.

"Stupid."

It's stupid that before we know what we're doing or why, we start down a track of doing things we don't really want to do, just for money, and then spend that money, and need more money, and have to do more things we don't really want to do to get it.

Every single step of our M.I.S.S.I.O.N. is about trying to stop that slide; but there's also a chance that you can stop it on day one, before you ever even have a job just for money ....

That's why it's important to know that getting a job is only one of the answers to getting income, and creating your own work is an equally important answer to consider.

It's a common practice these days to do some part-time work before finishing school or university. It's a good idea to find out whether you would like to do that kind of work when you need to do it full-time, for the rest of your life. You may find you like it, or that you really hate it very quickly.

The bad part of this is that the work is nearly always for someone else. Most people don't decide to do work for themselves, they decide that they want some money and so they get a job ... and begin the cycle of doing things they don't want to do with most of their time.

We should consider it our duty to ourselves to be our own boss at some point in our lives, and before it's too late. We should see if we enjoy not having a boss more than having one. We should see if we prefer time spent doing things we like better than time spent earning money.

If our whole lives felt like a holiday, maybe we wouldn't need to work in a better-paid job we don't like to save up more money to take a week of holiday. If we enjoyed our days more, maybe we wouldn't feel like telling ourselves we "earned" an expensive thing in the shops that won't give us nearly as much pleasure once it's in our house. Maybe we'd need a drink after work less, if work had been more fun. Maybe we'd be happy not to own things, because we would own our lives instead.

The Bad Things About Bad Jobs

That's not all. There are at least three further bad things about working for other people that I haven't mentioned yet ....

It's Not Your Job To Benefit

One positive of working for someone else is that you can be quite specialised in your work – other people will do things you might not be so good at. That's good. The bad part is that you probably won't get most of the benefit of that.

You see, the reason people who start businesses hire other people to do specialised jobs for them is not because those people will be happier doing those jobs. They couldn't care less. They want to capture the value of that specialisation that the worker isn't able to capture.

That means that if someone is prepared to pay you FN10 an hour to do something, and then has a bunch of extra things that they have to do on top of that cost (buy you a uniform, manage your payroll expenses, pay taxes for you, etc.) then the work you do must be worth at least FN20. If it wasn't, the business would lose money on you every hour you worked there, and would soon go bust. And then you wouldn't have a job anymore.

So maybe the work you do is worth even more than 2 times what you're being paid. Maybe it's worth 3 or 4 or 5 times. That way the company can hire a manager who does nothing else all day except make sure you're doing the right thing, and gets paid more than you for doing that.

When you work for someone else you won't get all the value of your work. You won't get most of it. You probably won't get half of it. You will probably get less than a quarter of it, or maybe even a tenth of it. You will get a tiny fraction, and the rest will go to your bosses and the owners of the company.

Every single job in the world means you are losing out to everyone above you. It's a great reason to work for yourself.

It's Not Your Job To Scale

The second extra negative is the lack of "scalability."

Remember that money isn't just time and energy. It can also be creativity and intelligence. You can create real value for people with your original ideas or the clever way you think, but if you work for a company, unless you are very lucky, you will only be paid for your time. Any great ideas you have will belong to the company.

Imagine you have an amazing idea for something that everyone in the world will want to buy, that will change their lives for the better. If you're working for a company, that's the company's idea. If you're working for yourself, it's yours.

And It's Just Not Your Job

To me, perhaps the most worrying thing about our entire world's focus on getting a job is that we have to wait for someone else to create that job for us. It means we start out not being in control, and so it is harder to take control later.

It means that someone else literally has to put everything else in place, just right, for that to be your dream job.

Because this isn't a fairy tale, the chances of that happening are very slim and, unfortunately, if such a job is created, lots of other people will try to get that job too!

If you really want a dream job – or even just a decent one – it's much more likely you can create it yourself than someone else will do it for you.

Back In The Real World – "Bulls#it Jobs"

How bad can it be? After that Gallup Poll in 2017 reported that 85% of people around the world dislike their jobs, David Graeber published the book *Bullshit Jobs*, which estimated that 2 out of 5 jobs have no chance of being interesting, because they shouldn't exist in the first place. They just happened by accident, or were deliberately invented to make someone else feel good, and hierarchical management structures don't want to remove them, because that will make managers feel bad.

Graeber lists 5 types of these jobs – flunkies, goons, duct-tapers, box-tickers and task-masters – but the nature of their task isn't important, apart from the fact that it just isn't important.

Graeber quotes psychologist Karl Groos who wrote all the way back in 1901 that babies gurgle with happiness when they shake a rattle because it is then that they discover their actions have a predictable impact on the outside world. Graeber takes it further to state that "a human being unable to have a meaningful impact on the world ceases to exist." It is part of being human to enjoy being able to influence the world around us. It is so hard-wired into our system that having influence makes babies grin, and not having an impact makes adults depressed.

We put in an input, we see an output, it gives us pleasure.

Except that when we're in a bulls#it job, we don't. We go to a job, we spend some time, we put in some input sometimes, we see no output. Sometimes we see negative feedback, which makes us dread putting in more input. The bullshit job can't give positive feedback, because it shouldn't exist.

This doesn't mean that our jobs need to be impressive, or have impressive titles. We may be able to find meaning in even the simplest of jobs; but if we don't, they will stop us finding our *Happy Ever After*.

Try working for other people at some point, and then try working for yourself: starting your own business so you don't get trapped in the cycle of spending all the money you earn in a job because you hate the job so much, and then become unable to escape.

And if you've already got a job, and can't take the risk of quitting to start a business just to see if you'd prefer it, then why not set up a little business on the side.

A side-gig ....

The Side-Gig Side Bar

Search the Internet, right now, for "side-gig" or "side-hustle" and see what comes up. You really should do it because, let's face it, if you're going to run a business on the side while still doing your day-job, you're going to have to be resourceful and energetic; and if you can't be bothered to google some ideas in the next minute or so, well, it's going to be hard going.

Before you do that, it's probably best to know what a side-gig is and, more importantly, why it is such a good idea.

First, and simply, a side-gig is any gig that is not your main gig. You do a main thing in your life. Your side-gig is not that. It's the other thing you do.

Let's say it's whatever you want it to be, particularly if the main thing in your life isn't everything you want it to be.

- It could be a gig that you happen to like that could make you a little extra money.

- It could be a gig you don't like much that makes you a lot of extra money.

- Or it could be a gig that hardly pays at all but might lead to bigger and better things.

Some Stories About Side-Gigs

Jill wanted to act. She had studied a little mime in her acting classes and thought that she could use that to make some extra money as an entertainer at children's parties. Let's imagine what might happen.

STORY 1: Jill learns some new skills, taking what she's done in a classroom and trying it in the real world. It helps her develop skills that are outside of her classwork and she becomes quite good as a result. And while she definitely couldn't plan for it, one day the parents at a party are from the film industry and want to hire her for something else. It could be the start of her dreams.

STORY 2: Jill is a genius at organising kids parties, and all kinds of other events, and she would never have known that if she hadn't tried. It becomes bigger, to the point where she hires other actors and teaches them how to do it, and eventually Jill becomes a world-leader at children's parties. It isn't what she started out wanting, but it made her a lot of money, became her main thing – and she enjoys it.

STORY 3. Maybe Jill was really good at it, even though she hated both it and the screaming spoiled kids she had to entertain. (What's wrong with Jill? She seemed so nice in the first two stories!) It's still a way for her to make money on the side, better than waitressing, while continuing to pursue her completely un-clown-like other dreams.

STORY 4. Or not. She does a few parties, and decides it really isn't for her, but it brought in some money that she wasn't going to get otherwise.

How Many Sides To a Side-Gig?

In reality, that last outcome is typical, but that's not a bad thing. You get some extra money, which helps you save. And as with even the most unsuccessful side-gigs, you learn something from it, even if the only thing you learn is that clowning isn't for you.

While entertaining kids is a pretty impressive side-gig, it doesn't have to be like that. It could be stacking shelves at a shop. It could be helping a friend's child practise reading. It could be developing your craft hobby to a level where you can sell your work at a local market or even online. It could be helping friends with their start-up business, looking through their accounts. It could be bigger or smaller than any of those.

You could develop a more moral twist to it, too, like helping the environment if that's something you care about – or a charity, or a favourite cause. You could restore old furniture that you pick up in dumps and junk shops and make them look really special. You could make old clothing look fashionable and new again.

If you want to supplement both the income and fulfillment you get from your main job, then a more interesting but also paying side-gig is the one for you. It could be in the form of a part-time job, but it is also a great opportunity to start up a little business, see how you enjoy it, and see whether it has real potential.

But if what you really want from the side-gig is the money, because you're not being paid enough in your current main gig to save up at the speed you want, then that is what you should focus on. Get paid and don't waste a cent of it.

The Invisible Side Benefit Of Side-Gigs

In fact, even a side-gig where you don't get much money coming in, and you do nothing but help other people, will help you reach your money goals better than not doing it – even if you can't see it happening. Done right, a side-gig should help you cut back on your spending and increase your saving.

1. It can stop you having free time in which you might be tempted to spend money. You might think that's not true, but think how it might take up evenings when you would otherwise go hang out with friends, maybe get a few drinks, or weekends when you might go to the shops, or a café … and the spending starts to kick in.

It might seem like a bad thing that side-gigs reduce your free time, but if your free time isn't "free," then that's a good thing. And you will probably make new friends in your side-gig too, possibly customers or fellow entrepreneurs who encourage you.

2. It gets you off the couch, doing things, achieving things, making you feel good about your life. It gets you away from advertising that tells you that the only thing that will make you feel better is to buy new stuff, because you're already getting the most valuable stuff elsewhere, the stuff that really makes you feel better: achievement.

From Side To Main

Side-gigs can become main gigs.

• It could be the thing that helps you move and develop your career in the direction you want it to go, by developing a skill that your job won't give you, or connections you otherwise couldn't get.

- It could be the thing that gives you the most satisfaction you get in your life, by helping other people or doing something you really want to do.

- It could be the way you try something new. That new thing might be something you love and want to switch to, or it might be something that you find out you actually don't like and you're lucky you didn't switch.

That last one might seem small, but it could be the biggest and best reason to get a side-gig. Too many people save up to quit their jobs with no experience of their new lives. A side-gig gives you the potential to make sure that this is the thing you really want to do.

Jill Saves On The Side

Let's say that Jill's side-gig did some of that. It brought in 7% extra money and it cut her spending by just 3%. Combined, that's an extra 10% to save a year, at the same time as she was growing and developing her skills and enjoying herself.

You might think that's not such a big deal, but 10% extra savings could seriously change her life.

- If Jill was earning FN20,000 a year and saving 15% (FN3,000), as we saw at the end of "M for Money," she should be free after 50 years. If she's 20 today, she might be 70 years old before she will be free.

- Jill's clowning side-gig could change that to earning FN21,400 (7% extra) and saving FN5,350 (25% instead of 15%, because she has less time to spend now, and more sense of achievement outside).

- She could be free after 36 years instead of 50, stopping work at 56 years old and not 70: 14 years of freedom from a small side-gig!

With just one small change to our lives, perhaps just a little bit of clowning around, we could increase our freedom and the best years of our lives.

So Many Side-Gig Solutions

Imagine what you could do on the side. Think about this as hard as you can. Pretty much everyone can do it.

At school and think you can't do this? You can do holiday jobs: tuition for younger kids – or even helping them with homework during their term-time.

Not academic? Help coach them for sport.

Working and still like sport? Become a part-time personal trainer. A lot of people who want a personal trainer don't have time during the day to meet a personal trainer, so doing it as a side-gig is ideal. You could start by offering to lead a group of people at work either right before or right after work or at lunch time.

My wife teaches yoga to her colleagues, at their office, once a week. She charges a little bit of money for it (just because they don't take it seriously otherwise), she gets to practise teaching yoga, and one of her colleagues told her, a couple of years' after starting, that it had changed her health and her life. It's a small side-gig, but it made a huge change.

All problems, looked at from a different perspective, have a solution. Find that solution through a side-gig and you will change your life by just changing the way you spend your spare time. And by giving up a little spare time now, you can create a huge amount of spare time later.

What do you enjoy? What are you good at? The Japanese use a term called *ikigai* to describe a combination of enjoying something, being good at it, being able to be paid for it and the world needing it. The Japanese believe that finding your *ikigai* will help you live longer and happier. If your job doesn't create *ikigai* for you, then maybe your side-gig will.

And just in case you really don't have time to google up some side-gig ideas, here's a website with 99 other ideas for you ...

http://www.sidehustlenation.com/ideas/

A Second Step Out Of The Woods

In the first stage of the MISSION – learning about money – we started to understand that money can be saved for when we need the time and energy more than we do today; and that if we started saving 15% of our income, we could be out of the woods by the age of 70.

It's better than never getting out of the woods, but only just.

Now that we've learned about income, and the potential importance of getting in a second or side-income to fast-track our savings, what can we save now? What if we can put aside 25%?

By increasing our saving from 15% to 25%, we can cut the number of years we need to work from 50 to 36, meaning that if we start saving at 20, we can be free at the age of 56 instead of 70.

If, right now, you're just about to leave school or university, that might not sound like such a big deal, because 58 and 72 both sound so far away.

Imagine instead that you have to go back to school for another 14 years. And not the fun bits of school either. You have to go back to the science class or to detention. To working in silence while the sun is shining outside.

If you could have been free at 56, but instead have to wait until 70, that's what it will feel like.

It could be a side-gig that makes all the difference.

Are You Ready To Make More Money?

Can you remember which parts of making more income are real, and which are make-believe?

1. **Is the job someone else has created likely to be my dream job?**

   a) Yes, because they're really nice people and have my best interests at heart.

   b) No, because the job isn't very nice, and they don't want to do it.

   c) No, because they can charge a lot more money for what I do with my time than they are paying me.

2. **Will you get the benefit of all the things you do in a job for someone else?**

   a) Yes.

   b) No.

   c) Not even nearly.

3. **What's the invisible side benefit of a side-gig?**

   a) Somewhere else to steal stationery from.

   b) No one will be able to see you while you're at work.

   c) Because you'll spend more time working, you won't be able to spend as much time spending money.

4. **Before Jill was clowning, she saved 15% of her income. In the example, how many years did this mean she had to work before achieving her Freedom Formula?**

   a) 60.

   b) 50.

   c) 40.

   d) 30.

5. **Her side-gig meant she could increase her saving from 15% to 25% of her income. How many years does she now need to work before achieving her formula?**

   a) 56.

   b) 46.

   c) 36.

   d) 26.

6. **If she doesn't save any of her money, when will she be free?**

   a) 98.

   b) 78.

   c) 58.

   d) Never.

7. **Name 100 possible side-gigs you could do.**

   a) Really, you should do this. The more you search, the more likely you are to find one for you.

Answers ...

1. b) Any job you are offered will either make the company money – or be something the boss doesn't want to do. Dream jobs are just dreams.
2. b)
3. c)
4. b)
5. c) 10% extra saving bought her 14 years of extra freedom.
6. d)

7. Now it's your turn to provide the answers. Once you've googled 100 different ideas, write 10 of the best ones here:

1) 6.

2) 7.

3) 8.

4) 9.

Free Income Stuff – *Side-Hustle School*

The best side-gig ever must have been *Harry Potter,* which JK Rowling wrote in her spare time, and made her one of the richest people in the world.

If you don't have an idea that magical just floating around, check out www.sidehustleschool.com, where author Chris Guillebeau will give you tons of tips, tricks and inspiration from real-life examples that will start you making extra money in your spare time sooner than you can say, "Akio money," or whatever spell JK Rowling used to become so rich.

Chris is an inspiration for real people looking for real alternative lifestyles, having also published books such as *The Art Of Non-Conformity* and *The $100 Start-Up*, which investigates micro-businesses, giving us confidence that entrepreneurship is something within all our grasps.

"You think dragons like jewellery?"

The Age Of Dragons
And Saving

"Do you know why your father sends princes to steal gold coins from the dragon?" Charlie asked the princess.

"Because any prince who wants my hand in marriage must prove himself to be both brave and clever," the princess replied, as though it were a line she had heard repeated a dozen times. Because she had.

"No," croaked Charlie. "It's because he knows that the princes who are stupid enough to attempt it will die trying, and the ones who aren't that stupid will just go away and never come back."

"Why not?"

"Because it's a dragon," said Charlie, as though that was the end of his answer, "and it wants to keep all that gold for itself. And why do you think dragons like gold so much?"

"Because it's shiny and it makes pretty jewellery."

"You think dragons like jewellery?" Charlie asked.

"Who doesn't?" asked the princess.

"Dragons don't care about jewellery," Charlie assured her. "Dragons save up gold because they live for a really, really, long time."

"How long?"

"Actually, no one knows, princess, because no one has ever seen a dragon die of old age. They only die on the rare occasion that a prince gets very lucky. Even dragons don't know how long they're going to live."

"But why does that mean they need to hoard so much gold?" asked the princess.

"That's a really good question, princess," Charlie said, thinking he might finally be making some progress. "Dragons need to save so much gold because they only know how to save, not how to invest, and because they don't know how long they're going to live, so they don't know how much they need to save," Charlie explained.

"But no one knows how long they're going to live ..." said the princess.

"That's right," said Charlie, "But we can use the magic of compounding to make our savings last forever."

The princess jumped up at the mention of the word magic. "Are we going to learn magic now?"

"No," Charlie said, disappointing the princess. "First we need to learn how to collect the things we use for that magic, savings, and how to protect them from the wicked witch of the worldwide web ...."

"Really?" asked the princess. "We are going to learn how to defeat wicked witches?"

"Really," Charlie said. "It's in the next chapter."

As they looked out of the window again, Charlie could tell that the princess was a little confused.

"Why did you say chapter?" asked the princess. "Are you getting all of this from some book?"

The Chapter 4
Cheat Sheet – Saving

How We Save More Money

1. Yes, we're going to say it again here: saving comes before spending!

2. Before you do anything else with your money, separate your saving from different types of spending. Use separate accounts and direct debits or even just envelopes. Whatever works to get savings away from spending.

3. You are saving for emergencies first, to get you through a disaster. Then you save for assets – an investment fund followed by some property – and once you've started doing that, you are saving for freedom.

4. You can fool yourself into saving more by saving half of any new money that comes in: half of any pay rise, side-gig or new job goes into your savings. Half for now, half for later. This works.

5. You can't trust other people to save for you, but you can use things like mortgages, insurance schemes and investment clubs to encourage you to save.

6. You should save as much as you can: it will bring you freedom faster. Target 20% of your income and build from there.

7. Try it out for just 30 days. After "Dry January" try "Frugal February" or "Save-tember." One month of really strong saving will boost your bank balance and show you how possible Freedom really can be.

CHAPTER 4
S For Saving

There are four words that will get you to *Happy Ever After* faster than any others: **saving comes before spending.** In the dictionary, in this book and in life too, saving comes before spending.

If you don't save before you spend, you won't save. Most people don't. You may sometimes manage to earn a bit more than you then spend, but that's not saving and it won't last – because it's accidental. If you don't learn to save before you spend, you'll increase your spending until it catches up with your income, so that your saving rate drops back to zero again. Even worse, you may spend more and have to start borrowing.

It's that straightforward.

Learn as soon as you can that saving creates freedom and that spending doesn't equal happiness. The more you save, the sooner you will be free; but spending more won't make you happier. Save first.

Why do we save?

All the most successful people know why they do the things they're successful at. We need to know our reasons too.

We save for these four things, in this order:

1. For emergencies.

2. For our first investment fund.

3. For (a deposit on) our first property.

4. For our Freedom Formula.

Become A Master Of Disaster

Don't underestimate emergencies.

One of the biggest causes of poverty is the impact of something going horribly wrong. The emergency could be a big natural disaster or global pandemic, or it could be a personal problem like illness, divorce or job-loss. When disaster strikes, people with no emergency money have to borrow, and it will be at the highest rates that can double their debt in no time at all. When a person with no savings needs money, everyone in that household suffers. That suffering can last a lifetime – even into following generations.

This is why the first and most important step towards being *Happy Ever After* is having an emergency fund.

Even if you don't think you're poor today, because you have a good job and a nice lifestyle, this could still mean you. People who earn good money but spend it all without saving for an emergency can drop into poverty just as quickly as someone on low income if something goes wrong.

It's the most important reason to save, and your "emergency fund" should eventually be around six months of your basic spending on rent, utilities and food, although three months of money is a good start.

It's not just about the bad times, either. It can help you make better choices. These could be riskier choices, like starting a business, or better choices, like waiting for a job offer you prefer.

It's like a safety net. Without a safety net, trapeze artists risk dying when they fall, so they can't take the same risks. Without an emergency fund, you can't risk not having work for a few months: even if it's not the job you really want, you have to take the job. You can't afford to wait to make the right decisions. And you definitely can't afford to take the risky decisions, because you might lose what little you have.

A few months of spending in the bank can mean saying no to a bad offer, riding out a bad run of luck, and waiting for a good offer to say yes. That's real power!

Saving For Investments

The second thing you save for are assets, things that will make money for you so that you no longer have to make it for yourself.

Once you have an emergency fund, you can start putting savings into higher risk and higher return assets.

Think of this, first and foremost, as saving for an investment fund. All the assets you buy, after your emergency fund, will be your investments. We will learn more about them later – in "I for Investing" – but for now you should just remember that your investment fund will include all your assets, your mutual funds, your exchange traded funds (ETFs), your bond funds and, yes, the house you will one day buy.

The Real Story Of The Avocado Toast Guy

Do you remember "the avocado toast guy"? He got in trouble for saying that young people actually do earn enough money to save up to buy a home, but instead they spend it on things like avocado toast.

"Is that true?" asked the princess. "If I just stop eating avocado toast I can save enough to never have to work?"

"I am sure I've already told you this isn't a fairy tale, princess," Charlie answered.

"Oh, that's a shame," sighed the princess, "because I don't even like avocados!"

There are a few good reasons "the avocado guy" (or Tim Gurner – to use his real name) got in trouble for saying this.

Obviously.

The first and really good reason was because what he said was wrong. Lots of people aren't saving because they can't cover their necessities, their basic food and rent, and they aren't wasting any money at all on avocado toast. Those people who never eat avocado toast got angry at being told – by a multi-millionaire – that the avocado toast they weren't eating was hurting their future.

The second reason he got in trouble, though, was because he was also kind of right – and the truth hurts. The truth hurts like hell, and hurt people get angry. For the people who were eating avocado toast and not saving, then it was their fault they weren't saving, and it still is. It isn't the millionaire's fault, and it certainly isn't the avocado's fault!

It isn't good to hear that it's your choice you aren't doing something you know you should be doing, but when it's a choice (unlike the people who can't afford the avocado in the first place), it's a choice that can be changed. Recognising the need for change is often the most painful part of change – but also the most necessary.

The third and probably most important reason he got in trouble was because he massively exaggerated the impact, saying you could buy a house with your avocado savings. That really didn't help. Saving on avocado toast isn't going to buy you a house anytime soon, and particularly not in Sydney, Australia, which is where he is from, because it is the world's most expensive property when compared to incomes – as well as being ground zero for avocado toast.

The median (the best way of measuring the average for this purpose) property in Sydney costs about 12.9X the median income, according to the International Housing Affordability Survey by think-tank demographia, meaning it would take 129 years of saving 10% of your salary to buy a house there. So even if you're spending 10% of your salary on avocado toast (why would you do that?), you would need to stop eating it for 129 years before it paid for a house.

That doesn't mean you should just give up though: if there's something you can give up, whether it's been smashed and served on sourdough or not, this will really boost your savings rate and help you build a meaningful investment portfolio.

Avocados on toast with coffee twice a week could add up to about US$50 in plenty of big cities, or US$2,600 a year. You're right to think that won't buy you a house, or even a deposit on a house, any time soon. Invested reasonably well, making a little bit over a 7% return, it will have doubled to about US$5,200 in 10 years' time. Still not a deposit, let alone a house.

Maintained as a habit, however, saving US$50 a week for that whole decade, invested at 7% a year, will get you almost US$39,000 dollars at the end of a decade. That will get you a deposit on a small house. Somewhere.

It might not be the house of your dreams, and it may not even be a house you want to live in, but it may be something you choose to rent out – your first investment property. Whatever it is, it will be better than not having US$39,000 and only memories of avocado.

Repeated over your whole working life, from 20 years old to 70, not eating avocados on toast and investing the money (at 7% annualised return) would build to US$1 million, just in time for your 70th birthday, if you start at 20.

Here's a chart we've borrowed from *The Thousand Dollar Journal,* my other book, to show what it looks like: 50 years of saving $50 a week and making investment gains of 7%.

Yes, really, you might be sacrificing a million dollars by buying avocado toast. Over your lifetime, spending just $50 a week on things you don't need could reduce your savings by a million dollars.

We can have two reactions to this.

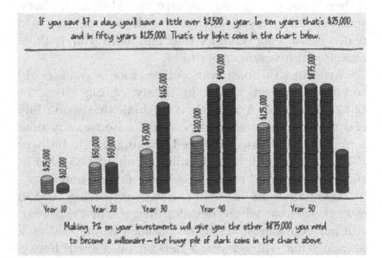

Figure 4.1

It's not nice to hear because it makes it our responsibility to save. It can be uncomfortable to hear that our choice to spend rather than save and invest has held back our freedom and hurt our chances of *Happy Ever After*, and that can feel unpleasant. We can feel regret about those choices, or even anger and denial.

It can also be empowering.

If it's our choice, we can change our choices. With the right information, and planning, we can change our ways. Even if the thing we're spending on is really small and won't change our lives immediately, it could change our habits; and if we learn the habit of saving, that will be enough change for now.

Saving For Freedom

Remember that back in "M for Money" we talked about this?

When we're young, we have time and energy, but no money.

When we're working, we have energy and money, but no time.

When we're old, we have money and time, but no energy.

We pointed out then that it sadly doesn't always work that way.

Some lucky young princes are born rich, and have money, time and energy when they're young, and it stays with them their whole life. Some other hardworking princesses make a lot of money quickly when they're working and retire young with enough money to live their life while they can still enjoy it.

More often it happens the other way though ....
Most people don't save enough money throughout their lives to retire or be free. They rely on their government, or on handouts, or on charity, or on their

families. Don't let this be you. That's not freedom. That's never being free.

That's why we save: to be free, not because we accidentally happen to have money left over after spending.

- We save because of emergencies, so that we can avoid dropping into poverty.

- We save because we will want to have some life left over after working, and we will want to enjoy it.

- We will want to be able to buy other people's time and energy in the future.

- But more than this, we save to be free.

Nothing we can buy will ever make us happier than freedom – and that's why we save. To be free.

Savings equals freedom. The more savings we have, the freer we are. The more we save, the sooner we will be free.

I needed to find this out for myself, as I had no idea what the point of saving was when I was younger. I had literally no money in my bank account at the end of every month until I was in my 30s with a couple of kids at home that needed feeding and clothing. I didn't see the point. Retirement was too far in the distance and buying a house seemed like an impossible dream. I can truly empathise with every millennial and my own Gen Z kids who despair of owning property, because I did too, and couldn't understand how even the first rung on the ladder was achievable.

I know it has become even harder.

Often saving just felt like I was delaying spending, buying later rather than buying it now. I didn't know why I should bother – because I didn't know saving could eventually buy freedom.

Saving can buy the ability to choose what we do with every minute we have left in our lives. To travel, to work for others – or not, to feel no stress, to party non-stop, to do nothing, to choose to do nothing, to choose to do something really difficult that may not work but may be amazing anyway ... to choose what makes us *Happy Ever After*.

That is why we save.

How do we save?

It's easy to think that "earn more and spend less" is the way to save more, just like "exercise more and eat less" sounds so right for losing weight and getting fit. But the reason why so many sensible diets don't work, and so few people have savings, is because the obvious solutions often don't work.

When you are trying to get fit and thin, you might decide to go for your longest run yet, making sure you get a few extra carbs in your system to keep you going beforehand – and take a couple of energy boosters with you and maybe a sports drink just in case? And then after the run, you're so happy with what you've achieved, and of course tired and hungry, that you eat an extra-large lunch to celebrate having done it ... and then, when you get around to weighing yourself, surprise, surprise, you've gained weight.

Most studies show that if you really want to start losing weight, you have to start by being strict about your eating, not just the totals but also how and when you eat them, and doing so in such a way that you can sustain the habit. And then, when you exercise, you have to make sure you don't go crazy celebrating in the kitchen. You have to have a plan to eat right and exercise right.

When you want to become free by saving, you can definitely focus on earning more money, but only with a focus on saving more. The reason to earn more is to save more.

There's no point working hard to get an extra FN1,000 a month, and then spending all of that on new things you couldn't afford before you earned it, only to find that you're exhausted after all this extra work, can't keep doing it, and so stop doing it, but now with a higher expected standard of living.

Most consumer companies have a plan that exploits this habit, and even try to create it, called "premiumisation." Take a basic product, add something different to it, maybe just a different label or slightly different ingredient, and sell it for a much higher price. People who have more money will be tempted to buy it just because it is different and more expensive, so they will look richer (and therefore cleverer) than their friends by buying it. Don't fall into this trap!

You may even repeat the advertising taglines to yourself, that you "earned it," and that you're "worth it," which is true. You earned the money, and you're worth much more than the corny sales line. You have earned some freedom and you will be worth it – as long as you save it.

Working harder to spend more money is the opposite of what we want to achieve. If you're going to earn more, you need to plan to save more of it right from the very start.

How you save will depend on your circumstances. You may get paid in cash or directly to the bank, either weekly or monthly. You may get annual or half-yearly bonuses that are easier to save, but also easier to spend on wasteful luxury goods. You may have a business that blows hot and cold, or you may be saying to yourself that you just don't earn enough money to save right now.

Here are a few strategies, tactics and secret little tips that will help you deal with all of those situations and more. Try them all and see which work best for you.

1. The envelope method

If you get paid in cash, don't keep all of your money in one place, because then your savings will mix with your spending and will never get saved. Get four or five envelopes, preferably in different colours but even more preferably for free by using old ones, and then label them with these words.

- saving

- rent/utilities

- food

- paying off debts/education

- enjoyment.

Then you put into each envelope the amount of money you want to go to those items until you get paid again. First comes savings (remember!), then rent and utilities (shelter and warmth), food, some money to pay off your debts if you have any, and then, finally, anything else is enjoyment.

Yes. The savings envelope comes first. Saving always comes first.

2. The direct debit method

If envelopes stuffed with cash seems a little old world to you, then you can do exactly the same thing with bank accounts. It's less physical, which can make it feel less real, but in some ways more efficient.

You can open more than one bank account. You can open different accounts pretty much free of charge if you do it right. Then you can use these accounts exactly like you use the envelopes. You don't need all five, or however many envelopes you had, but you can get the bank to automate your saving for you by direct debit.

So, you open a savings account that doesn't have an ATM card – or you throw the ATM card away – and then arrange a direct debit from your current account, or wherever your income goes, to that account. The key is for it to be as untouchable as possible, so it remains untouched. For now. We will do fun stuff with it later.

You then do the same with all of the other "envelope" spending categories as necessary. Set up a direct debit for your rent to be paid from your current account. Direct debit your utilities from that account too.

This should be painless, and much easier than the envelope method. With the envelope method, you have to repeat the process of putting money in the envelope every week or month. With direct debit, you don't even see it being done. You just have to be brave once and tell the bank to do the hard work for you. Once done, you can forget about it and get on with your life.

You can even set up those accounts to wire money automatically to investment accounts, market funds, etc., the same amount every month, so you don't just save automatically, you invest automatically too. You can then use one of the cleverest investment strategies out there – the "dollar-cost averaging" method – where you invest the same amount of money every month, meaning you buy more when things are cheap and less when they're expensive.

We discuss dollar-cost averaging in "I for Investing", but other than that, the envelope method and direct debit method are roughly the same, for the same kind of income that comes in regularly, every week or every month.

2a. Good Plastic or No Plastic

Good plastic. Once you have decided how much you can spend every month, you can then pay that money into an account that has a debit card, or put it onto a pre-paid debit card. That way, you can't spend any more than that. That's it. No more.

If you can't get a prepaid debit card, or a debit card that attaches to an account that you can limit to only a certain amount of spending per month, then you could switch back to the envelope method. Have no cards at all, and only spend what is in that envelope. Aim to have something left at the end of every period and add that extra back to your savings.

Keep score, to see what your best month is, and if you can beat it.

No plastic. Otherwise, used without this level of discipline, credit and debit cards are a really bad idea. Everyone spends more with them, because even worse than the emperor's new money, plastic doesn't feel like real money. Plus, if you only have cash, you can't buy stuff you don't have enough cash for, while credit cards will let you spend, spend, spend. Use plastic, or any other "easy payment" system, only to your advantage to manage your budget and help your saving.

3. Bonuses and businesses

People who work in jobs that pay a basic minimum salary, delaying a big chunk of income to a bonus or commission payment, will often tell themselves that they don't need to save any of their salary, as they will live on that and then save their bonus. But then they see something expensive they want to buy, and line that up for their bonus payment. Or they want to buy something special for someone else, a birthday treat or holiday ... and buy it before they get their bonus.

And when their bonus payment wasn't as big as they thought it was going to be, making them unhappy, they spend the smaller bonus payment on making themselves happy, and their saving comes last. And when saving comes last, it doesn't come at all.

Remember. Savings comes before spending, not just in monthly income but in bonuses, so anyone earning in that structure should make sure they can save something, no matter how little, out of their monthly income.

This is true for businesses too as they pay bonuses out of profits, which can only really come at the end of the year, and can be big, small or even negative. Saving there should be done monthly too.

It can be hard, but done right this kind of saving can be easier. It can also be done more effectively, because we have two opportunities to save, not just one.

We can still use the envelope/direct debit monthly method, and we should. Even if there isn't much money coming in, try to learn the habit of saving 5% or 10% every week or month so that we're really used to it by the time our big payday comes in. This way, we can look forward to our big payday really topping up the hard work we've been doing all year.

If you don't do the direct debit, or envelope or some kind of regular saving, there is a big chance that you also won't do the second kind of saving, which will mean you do none at all.

The second type of saving is the lump sum. This is where you take as much of the bonus or profit payment as you possibly can and put it into some kind of savings vehicle.

Read that again. As. Much. As. Possible.

What? No fun at all?

Ok, maybe this is where you can have some fun, but you've got to work out what kinds of things you can really save that might be fun.

Seven Ways To Make One-Off Saving More Fun

1. If your emergency fund isn't fully funded, then your money has to go there first. Calculate the minimum your emergency fund needs to be (three times your monthly spending is the very minimum for most people), and then keep track of how close you're getting. Make it a target, say FN6,000, and then download an app on your phone or draw in a marker pen on your fridge how close you're getting. Track your progress weekly and monthly until it's done.

2. You may find diversifying your emergency fund makes it more enjoyable, adding in some gold bars or silver coins in case of a real emergency, like a zombie apocalypse. A couple of silver coins in your sock drawer might only set you back a hundred dollars or less, depending on the price of silver, but it's money saved, and I have to admit it makes me feel like a pirate whenever I see them.

3. Buy the whole market. Index funds or cheap "exchange traded funds" (ETFs) buy hundreds of companies for you at a time, meaning that you own huge chunks of the economy. Before you do buy them, do research to find out which ones are best, which are cheapest, and which hold real assets. Doing this will add some diversification into your portfolio, and you'll find out new things – and that learning should come for free.

4. Make it more specific. Open a broker account and buy some shares in some safe companies. If you have a favourite drink, or meal or skincare product, think about buying shares in the company that makes it. Make one of the world's highest paid CEOs work for you and send them questions to answer at the company shareholders' meeting.

5. Buy something valuable and, most importantly, tradable. Make sure you can sell it back for at least as much as you paid for it, if not more when the market goes up in price: for example gold, but never diamonds (which sell for half their retail price at best!).

6. How about a one-off insurance product for your child's education? Not a bad idea, if you check the small print to make sure you can cancel, and that you're not paying too much as commission. It's a way of increasing your savings and feeling good about it too.

7. A house? Yeah, that would have to be a pretty big bonus, even to make the smallest deposit. But don't restrict your thinking to just your dream house – think about the opposite. Find out how much the cheapest property anywhere near you costs, and then find out what it would

cost to rent out. Is there a trade there? You shouldn't care if it's a garage, if you can rent it out at a high price this might be the start of your property empire! (We'll talk about "house-hacking" later.)

If you've got expensive debt, though, the best thing to do is pay it off. If that doesn't feel like fun, check out our snowball and avalanche methods in later pages and see if you can use this bonus to start a debt avalanche.

Whatever you do, though, don't use a windfall to buy a fancy car, or go on a "once-in-a-lifetime holiday" (they tend to become more regular than their name suggests). Don't give it to someone else. Don't waste it.

If your money comes in irregular chunks, rather than a reliable salary, you have the opportunity to use it to make your saving easier and your life free by putting it somewhere you can't spend it, in one quick go, rather than forcing yourself to do the hard work every single day of the week and month of the year.

You also have the risk that you may save nothing all that year – and then blow your windfall in one go! And that's why you should use both methods, both regular and random, to make sure you get some saving done and get yourself in the habit.

A Little Help ...

It's difficult to get good help with your saving. Really smart advisors are likely to be very expensive. Advisors that promise to be very cheap or even free are a concern – they may be a scam.

There are schemes you can use to help you though, if you think it would be useful. Mortgages and life insurance charge money for what they give you, but they have one factor that you can use which helps them work time after time advisors.

The Persuasion Factor

Whether it's moral, social or financial persuasion, whoever is running this system will have leverage over you to make sure you pay up. Which means you save.

If you don't pay your mortgage, your house might get taken away and you end up out on the street. That's some serious motivation to pay money into the bank every month.

If you don't pay your insurance premium, the policy could get cancelled and you could lose the whole value of it, everything you have put in so far. Again, great motivation to keep on paying in and therefore save.

Don't think this comes for free, though. This is how banks and insurance companies make money, and they're big industries, so they're making a lot of money from this.

The interest rate on the mortgage will mean that you eventually pay back much more than you borrow. For example, even if the interest rate is only 3.5%, over the space of 20 years, the amount you have to pay back will double: if you borrow FN100,000 for 20 years, you pay back FN200,000 in a 20-year mortgage at 3.5%.

Now that's ok if the value of your house goes from FN100,000 to FN300,000, which does happen at times, but they also sometimes stay flat or go down. If that's the case, you should make sure that a mortgage payment isn't your only form of saving.

A life insurance premium is another method, although you will undoubtedly end up with less than you could have got by doing this yourself. The fact that a lot of the first few years' worth of life insurance premiums go to paying the salesperson's commission should make that pretty obvious. But if you aren't going to be able to save without some help, then saving something is better than nothing.

These days, you can find a lot of interesting cheaper policies online, where you should be able to get the same end result by putting in less money and not paying so much sales commission. Try to find those.

If you really find it difficult to put money into a savings account yourself, and keep it there, then these are all valid ways of starting to separate the money you want to use in the future from the money you want to use today. If you need that help, then use other people's programmes. It may not be the most efficient, but it will get something saved, and something inefficient is definitely better than nothing, no matter how efficient that nothing is.

How much should we save?

The most common recommendation for how much to save is 20% of your annual or monthly income. It's a good starting point, but take another look at this chart:

It shows the relationship between how much you save and how long you need to work. Across the bottom is the percentage of your income that you save, and on the left-hand side the numbers of years you will need to work, if that's how much you save.

The two extremes are important because they are indisputable. Starting on the left, if you don't save and no one else saves for you, you will have to work until you die – or 100 on this chart.

On the far right, if you save 100% of your income you can stop working right now, if you like, because

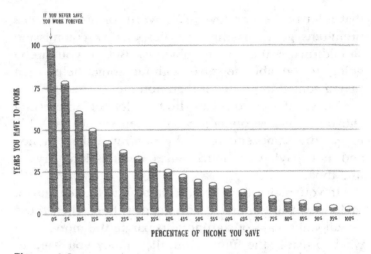

Figure 4.2

you clearly don't need any money to spend. That's silly, and extreme, but it's also logically true.

All the bars in between show how long your career needs to be depending on the percentage of your income that you save. If you save 10%, you will need to work until you're 80 years old, and saving 20% will enable you to stop work around 60 years old.

But what if we wanted to live free for more of our life than this?

So, let's ask that question instead: rather than asking how much is the right amount to save, let's ask how much of our adult lives we want free:

- Half of it, stopping work at 50 (if we live to 80)?

- Three quarters, stopping work at 35?

Look at the chart, and see what that tells you about the amount you need to save. To stop working around 50, you will have to save something like 30% of your income, if you can get a 7% return on your investments. Which you can.

To stop working in your mid to late 30s, you will need to save about half of your income. Now, how much do you think you should save?

Saving For Freedom: A Rough Guide

1. **Saving 0% of your income will get you 0% freedom** in your adult life. It's obvious but it's still what so many people are doing. Assuming that rich people are doing a lot of the saving (because they have most of the money), a lot of people are not saving at all, and so will get 0% freedom.

2. **Saving 10% of your income could set you free by 80.** If your investments earn you a 7% return with 3% inflation you could be free by 80, but not a lot before then. Sorry.

3. **Save 20% and you could be free by 62.** If you live to 80, that's 18 years of freedom, or more than a third of your adult life without having to work. Now it's starting to get interesting ...

4. **Save 30% of your income and you could be free by 52.** Again, based on 7% investment returns, half your adult life could be free.

5. **Saving 40% of your income and you'll be free by 44:** 24 years of work and the rest of your life free by saving 40% of your income.

6. **Save 50% and well ... well done you!** With the same returns as above, you should be free by your mid to late 30s, but with that kind of saving, you might fancy investing in higher return investments and shortening your time at work even more.

7. **Some people do it in less than 10 years.** Can you?

Trick Yourself Into Saving More

If you've just started working, if you're earning some-thing close to minimum wage, those numbers above might feel really over-optimistic. If you feel you can't save anything at all, let alone the 50% we just talked about, then try this:

- Start saving now, just the tiniest amount, what-ever you can afford, just to get in the habit.

- Then save 50% of every pay rise you ever get.

- Save 50% of all side-hustle money you make.

- Save 50% of any extra money you ever get.

This will get you there. Maybe not immediately, but sooner than you think.

Importantly, when you get new money that you haven't become used to spending, it's easier to save. You're not giving anything up, you're just not add-ing anything new, so it will be easier to save. And it can work like a ladder, adding incrementally to your total saving and the speed with which you're adding to your total.

If you earn FN1,000 a month, and only save FN50, that's 5%. It's not enough. You may not be free before 80.

If you get a 10% pay increase, spending the other half, that's another FN50 saved. All of a sudden, you're saving nearer 10% of your income, and you should be free around 70. It's not amazing, but it's better than 80.

Then if you start a side-gig, and that makes you another FN100, saving another 50 will bump you up to FN150 a month, and you'll be at three times your origi-nal saving rate.

Why do it this way?

If FN1,000 is just enough for you to get by, and FN50 is the maximum level you're comfortable saving, then it will be painful, tough or even impossible to cut back your spending by FN100 to save FN150. And if you manage it for one month, or even two, you might stop soon after, and then it won't change your life.

If you start saving when new money comes in, however, then you haven't become used to spending it. It won't be painful to take it out of the total, because it wasn't there before.

By increasing your saving rate from 5% to nearer 15% you have tripled the rate at which you are accumulating savings, and this will change your life with the least amount of pain.

It shouldn't be just a one-time thing. You should do this for every single increase you get. Let's say, over time, you steadily increase the amount of money you get in from your side-gigs, and regular job, so that your total income has doubled from the FN1,000 per month, to FN2,000 a month.

If you stick to this rule, then half of that extra FN1,000 will be saved, which means that your savings will have gone from FN50 per month, or 5%, to FN550, or 27.5%, which will make you free as early as 48!

That's not all. Because you have only saved half of every income increase, your spending will have increased at the same time, from FN950 to FN1,450, an increase of more than 50%, so it should feel like you live a richer life too.

One for now, one for later

This works because, like so many things that work, it's simple and easy to follow. The rule itself really couldn't be easier: "one for now and one for later".

The rule reminds me of childhood summers spent at pick-your-own strawberry farms, where one strawberry would go in the basket to be weighed and paid for, and the next one would go straight in my mouth when the farmer wasn't watching! One for now, and one for later.

With this rule, I got some fun and the farmer got some money for the strawberries I hadn't eaten. Without the rule, it would have been all work and no fun, or all fun and I would be both sick and in trouble. Sound familiar?

By taking out half of any increase in income, you are getting the best of both worlds. You are increasing your savings by a substantial amount, and you are increasing your ability to spend by a significant amount too, to help you enjoy "living in the moment."

Because it's simple, it's easy to stick to; and because you can stick to it, it can create long-term change. That's why it works. This way allows you to increase your saving and increase your spending at the same time. What could be better than that!?

In the real world, it may not work out to be exactly 50% of every single increase. Some increases may come in faster than this, when you don't need them, and you may be able to save them all. You should do that.

Some may come in more slowly, and your spending needs may have increased over time, so it will be difficult to add the whole 50% to savings, but you should try to do your best.

Over time, as your income increases from FN1,000 to FN2,000 to maybe even FN5,000, you may find you are able to keep close to that 50% number. If you do, at FN5,000, you will be saving FN2,000, 50% of the increase from FN1,000 and 40% of your income. If you average that over your working life, then you may have to work only 20 years, leaving you free to do whatever you want for the rest of your life.

That sounds a lot better than 5%. And it shows what you can achieve by starting small and early.

(If there's one thing I regret in this book, a lesson that I didn't follow personally, it is this one. Someone told me to do this when I was in my early 20s, and I didn't listen. I had a freelance kind of income, I didn't get pay increases, as such, so I didn't listen. I should have. I would have been free 10 years ago, if not sooner.)

What are you saving for?

It's a good idea to remember the things you're saving for, not just to give you motivation to save for it, but maybe also to change the way you save.

At the beginning of this stage of the M.I.S.S.I.O.N., we pointed out the four phases of saving, or reasons to save. You save for your

1. emergency fund

2. investment fund

3. property fund

4. freedom.

You can save for each of these reasons one at a time, but you can also build savings strategies around these reasons that may help you save a little bit more, as many people feel they can save more if they are breaking their savings up into different "pots" rather than just one big one.

As a simple example, some people might find it very difficult to put 20% of their salary every month into savings, but find it possible to put 8% into their retirement fund, 7% into saving for a down payment on their house and 5% into their emergency fund (adding up to 20%).

This can also be easier or more successful if the method of saving is different for each one. For example, your retirement fund could be a direct debit to an asset manager or broker that manages your investment for you. Your savings for a house deposit could be directed into your savings account, and your emergency fund could be in gold coins buried in the garden!

So try it. Try to think about saving for different things in different ways and see if it helps you to save more. (Saving for a holiday doesn't count, by the way. That is just spending!)

And remember ...

Saving is NOT what you have left after you spend. Saving does not come second to spending in this book, in the dictionary or in life. Saving comes first.

Cutting Back The Woods A Third Time

In the second stage of the M.I.S.S.I.O.N., we learned about increasing our income so we could increase the amount we save from 15% of our income to 25%, and as a result we bring forward the age at which we are financially independent, out of the woods, from 70 to 56.

That's not bad. It's not scary, and it is a lot better than most people manage to do. We can do better though, particularly now we know how. We can get out faster.

In this third stage of the M.I.S.S.I.O.N., we've learned about savings and how important they can really be. So what will our woods look like if we increase our savings rate from 25% to 35%?

Can you see the difference? Half of our adult life is now in the sunshine.

If we can save 35% of our income, we could cut our lifetime of working for money down another 8 years, from 36 years to 28 years, meaning we are free at 48 instead of 56.

How good does that sound?

To this 50-year-old at the time of writing, stopping a few years ago sounds pretty good!

Free Saving Stuff – www.sevendollarmillionaire.com

"What's the smallest amount of money you need to save every day, invested at a reasonable rate, to become a millionaire?"

That's the question my teenaged daughter asked me when I was starting to teach her about saving and investing. I thought it was a great question – but the answer was even better.

- Only seven dollars!

- Saved seven days a week,

- invested for 7% average annual returns,

- will give you seven-figure wealth,

- before you turn 70.

It's true. Save seven dollars a day from the age of 20, and start investing it well, and you'll be a millionaire by retirement. That's how small an amount of money you need to save.

The chart above shows how it happens. The light coins are your daily savings: $7 a day, $2,500 a year, $25,000 a decade. By year 50, that makes $125,000: better than zero, but not a million! Investing that money for 7% returns makes the other $875,000 you need to become a millionaire.

Have a look at our website www.sevendollarmillionaire.com for more tips on how to save and invest.

The website also features a page called "Start Here," to provide some practical advice on where and how to start saving and investing. We would have loved to put that all in this book, but that information can change by country and over time, so we update the "Start Here" page regularly: www.sevendollarmillionaire.com/start-here.

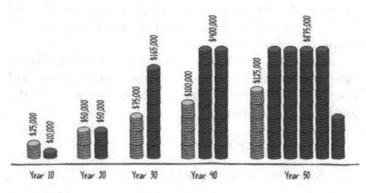

Figure 4.3

Do You Know How Saving Makes You *Happy Ever After?*

Can you save yourself from the wrong answers?

1. Which comes first?

  a) Saving.

  b) Spending.

2. How many months of spending do you need to have in an emergency fund?

  a) Three months.

  b) Six months.

  c) A year.

3. After you've saved for an emergency fund, what do you save for next? Put the following in the correct order:

  a) Your next holiday.

  b) Investing.

  c) Pay off credit card debt.

  d) A new bigger house.

4. How can you fool yourself into saving more money?

  a) Pretending you are saving, but then actually spending.

  b) Putting newspaper in the saving envelope and taking that to the bank.

  c) Saving half of every income increase you ever get, so you don't become used to spending more money.

  d) Imagining you have more money than you do.

5. Is it ok to keep the money you are saving with the money you will spend?

  a) Yes.

  b) No.

  c) No.

  d) No.

6. People who get bonuses, commission or have irregular income don't need to save regularly because one day they will get lucky and that will be enough.

  a) True.

  b) False.

  c) False (but widely believed).

7. Which of the following is not a good way of saving?

  a) Putting cash in an envelope and then putting it into a savings account at the bank.

  b) Buying gold.

  c) Getting a direct debit from your current account to your savings account.

  d) Promising you will start tomorrow.

Answers

1. Saving. Saving always comes first.
2. Three months is a minimum emergency fund and six months is probably ideal. Nine months might be excessive.

3. c) Pay off credit card debt first, then b) you can invest. After that, you can d) save for a new bigger house, but a) holidays are just spending.
4. c) One for now and one for later.
5. Always separate your saving money from your spending money, otherwise it will get spent.
6. Bonuses might help you save, but everyone should save monthly.
7. d) Tomorrow never comes. Saving starts today.

Back In The Real World ... Save-tember!

Try a 30-day challenge to save as much as you can.

Sometimes it can be fear of the long-range goal that stops us shooting for the near-term one. We can be so scared or dismissive of the big picture that we can't even look at the smaller one.

Sometimes when we talk about reducing our spending for the rest of our lives, it can sound really hard. We know there are a few things we can go without, but it might seem too daunting to go without all of them forever.

Instead, just for a while, stop thinking about *Happy Ever After* and start thinking about **Saving Right Now.** Just for a month. Just for this month, or next month, try to spend as little as you can. Cut back on everything you know can really be cut back on. It's only for a month ...

Map it out, day by day, week by week, what you can cut, where and when, and what else you can do instead of spending that money. Calculate how much you think is the maximum you can save, and then aim for it. Go for it with everything you've got and don't hold back at all.

Treat it like drinkers treat "Dry January." You need this like drinkers need a break. Spending is like drinking too, because the spending isn't worth the hangover! Maybe follow Dry January with Frugal February.

At the end of the month, divide how much you saved by your salary, to see what percentage of your income you saved.

If the timing works, you could even try to combine it with Dry January, as not spending on drinking will be a big advantage for some people. But don't wait for January if that's more than a few months away – you should do it soon. Next month at the very latest.

You could encourage some of your friends to join you, because they might want to save some money too. It could be just the support you need, or even a little friendly competition to see who can save the most (as a percentage of their income).

Telling friends and family also creates social pressure in the same way that public diet programmes create pressure to stop eating.

The worst that can happen is that you hate it and you don't save much money. Not good, but it's only for a month.

The best that can happen is that you love it. That you realise the mindless spending you've been doing hasn't been making you happy, but instead has been making you sad and holding you back from achieving your dreams.

If it feels very difficult, but got you saving much more than usual, maybe you could have a few saving months per year to boost your overall savings rate. Better yet, you could decide that it wasn't too hard and that you can actually cut back on lots of spending all the time. All that, in one month, plus a bit more money in the bank.

Make next month Frugal February, or Minimal March, No-Spending-vember or Save-tember. You don't need a silly name – just challenge yourself to save.

"Should I 'like' this, Charlie?"

The Wicked Witch
Of The Worldwide Web

"Far away, princess, in a realm much less magical than ours, a wicked witch has cast a terrible spell," explained Charlie.

"What kind of spell?" asked the princess. "Do all the princesses in the world fall asleep until they are kissed by a handsome prince?"

"No, princess. This spell affects everyone in the country, not just princesses," explained Charlie. "She has cast a net wide across the land that constantly sends all the people images of amazing and beautiful things they can buy, updating it with new information, new images, new everything ..."

"Actually Charlie, that doesn't really sound so bad," said the princess.

"It's not supposed to sound bad. It's supposed to sound wonderful. It's supposed to sound almost like magic, like something you wouldn't believe was possible only years before ..."

"Exactly ..." said the princess, confused.

"If it sounded bad, people wouldn't want it. They wouldn't want to get caught up in it. By showing them all these wonderful things, the wicked witch makes people want them more and more. She constantly shows people things they can't afford, things they don't need

but look lovely on the net, and so they always want to spend all of their money and can never save any of it."

"Ok," said the princess, still not totally sure why this was so bad.

"And so the people become trapped, working for weeks and months or even years to buy things they hadn't wanted before the web showed them. It means people are never really happy, because the witch makes sure that her net is constantly showing them new things they don't have, new things they believe might make them happy this time. They crave things they didn't know about just seconds before. The witch's spell is like a spider's web, a worldwide spider's web, that has caught all of the people in its invisible strands, so they can't escape," said Charlie.

"How can they escape? Do they need a knight in shining armour with a sharp sword to cut through the strands?"

"No, even that wouldn't work. It's actually much simpler than that, but also much harder. All they have to do is not want to be in the web."

"But that's so easy," said the princess. "Who would want to be in a web?"

"They do," said Charlie. "That's how evil the witch's spell is. Everyone wants to be in the web all the time, connected to all the other people in the web, even if it means spending all their money and never being free."

"Well, let's never go there then," concluded the princess, at which point a pinging noise came from under a cushion.

Charlie looked at her ...

"Oh," said the princess. "That web."

The Chapter 5 Cheat Sheet

How We Spend Less Money

1. Once you've saved 20% of your income, you can spend 50% on your basics and 30% on enjoyment and be free by 62, which is better than most people. Aim to save 44% by spending 44% on basics and 20% on enjoyment, and you could be free by 44!

2. Try to spend less than 30% on housing. Cut it back where you can. Don't get caught up in the game of thinking you can express your taste and personality through your house or any other spending. You can express your personality much better when you are free!

3. Arbitrage is paying less for the same thing. Opportunities for this exist everywhere: in vouchers, in restaurants, holidays and bulk buys.

4. Negotiate to win. Whenever you can (which is almost always), ask for a discount. Get competing bids and ask for the cheapest, and then repeat that to the next cheapest.

5. Research should put you in charge of pricing, not tell you what things you like the most and so have to pay more for.

6. Find ways to have fun not spending. Minimalism, stoicism, meditation and loads of ways of exercising are all popular trends that should be free and can reduce your spending. There will be lots more you can find if you look. Don't give away your money for nothing.

7. There are seven things you should cut back on right away – easy wins for easy savings.

CHAPTER 5
S For Spending

Some people, who put spending ahead of saving, who spend money all month and hope they have some left before the next cheque comes in, think that the way to save is to learn to spend less. Or at least to learn how to spend less crazily.

Now that you have put saving first, and spending second, you know that this isn't true. Your saving for the month is done first. It's there, in the bank, before you've done anything else ... so now you can go ahead and spend just as crazily as you like, with what's left.

If that's what you really want.

If you promise not to touch those savings.

If you think that will make you feel better about saving and encourage you to save more in the future.

Which it might, but probably won't for long.

Then come back here and read about how budgeting and spending sensibly will actually make your life much more enjoyable. How it will help you have more money left over. How it will enable you to focus on what really matters, not what marketing, online advertising, store displays, peer pressure, social media and everything else is distracting you with today.

"50 – 30 – 20": or should that be "20 – 50 – 30"?

If you look up online how to budget, you will most likely see three numbers. 50, 30 and 20, that add up to 100, that is 100% of your income.

So 50% is the amount of income this theory says you should budget spending on the basic cost of living, your rent, your utility bills – like electricity, water, phone – and maybe even your most basic food needs. Not your desire for high-end Italian cuisine or late-night drive-thru burgers: we do mean survival needs here.

And 30% is the amount you spend enjoying yourself: travel, entertainment, beers, restaurants, splurge food, fashion, paid sport events, theatre trips ... whatever it is you enjoy.

And 20% is the amount you save.

You already know what's wrong with this, don't you? Or you do if you remember that "Saving always comes before spending." Saving comes out of your income before anything else, so we need to correct that right away: the "20," if it is going to be "20," should come at the front, because saving always comes before spending.

Otherwise, the theory isn't too bad. It's a good start, but it could be better.

1. Yes, you should be targeting spending no more than 50% of your income level on your basic needs. Rent, essential food, electricity, etc.

2. Yes, you can, if you want, spend up to 30% of your life on non-essential enjoyment.

3. But if you want to increase the amount of money you save and fast-track your freedom, this is where the extra will have to come from. So it's fun money, but it's also the extra money, the money that will change your life.

So yes, we could write it ... 20 savings – 50 basics – 30 fun ...

As long as we know that if we work harder and smarter, it could be 30 savings – 50 basics – 20 fun ...

Or even 40 savings – 40 basics – 20 fun!

Then we would have an extra 10 or 20 to push into our savings the next month. Remember, that while a 20% savings rate will get you financial freedom around 62 years old, a 40% savings rate will achieve it at 44 years of age.

As we've already dealt with saving, and that 20% or more is already in our savings account, let's look at the big number first: the 50% for basics.

The (Basic) Cost of Living

1. Home and The Price of Freedom

When we leave home, we do it for the ability to choose what we do, and when we want to do it. It's a big part of freedom, having our own place. Unfortunately, no one, except parents (and other charities), hands out free accommodation, so we will need to pay for ours. This is our biggest and most important expense and it takes some real thought about where we should live and how much we want to spend on it.

There's no point saving a couple of cents with coupons every week if you're splurging hundreds of dollars too much on rent. It will never add up to freedom. Your accommodation will control your life.

Before you think about any other type of spending, think about this: where you live, the size and the location, and whether you rent it or own it, will probably be the biggest spending question you ask yourself every year; so ask it. Ask it properly.

Don't settle for expensive. Don't settle for the house of your dreams. Don't settle for upgrading.

That's too easy. This is where you can make the most impact to your life.

How much should you pay to live somewhere? The range of choice is enormous enough to be truly confusing. If you look hard enough you can probably find somewhere pretty close to free (although it might be a tent), and you can probably find somewhere else that is hundreds of times your income, because crazy rich people like to spend that kind of crazy money on rent.

I was lucky. When I started out, someone told me that you shouldn't spend more than one third of your income on rent. I didn't know why, but it seemed like a good number, so I followed it. When possible, I tried to get it below a quarter, but that can be pretty hard, and occasionally I managed below a fifth – but one third is a good number to start with.

It's a good number because if you pay around 30% of your income on rent, a bit less than a third, you have a decent chance of saving a meaningful portion of your income. You can spend another 20% on food, utilities, transport and the really essential things in life and still spend the 30% you need to enjoy yourself (**after** you've saved 20%).

If your rent is above 30% of your income, and is closer to 50% or even more, then your utilities and food are likely to eat up a good chunk of the 30% target and you will find yourself faced with a direct choice between fun and saving. This will make it much harder to save. Between fun and saving, most of the world generally, and not surprisingly, chooses fun.

So, what do you do if your rent is more than 30%?

You move house or change job. Seriously. You re-think your life.

Ask yourself if you need such a fancy place, or big place, or in such an expensive area. Your dream home doesn't belong in your reality, it belongs in your dreams. This isn't a fairy tale, remember?

Once you've saved enough money to be free, then decide if you want to spend some more time working to be free in your dream home. If you do the numbers right, you'll probably decide not to, because the real dream is being free.

Ask yourself if it needs to be so big or so central. Do some research and work out what else you can do. Accommodation, whether owned or rented, is everyone's biggest expense, and so it is really important to make the right decision. Bargain hard with your landlord or be prepared to move to a place where you are paying 30% or less.

If you can't get your rent below 30% of your income, you only really have two other options. One is to get a better job, or a second job, that can increase your total income to the point where rent is less than 30% again and you can save 20% or more. Or the other is to share the place you're getting with a friend to get the total cost you are paying back below 30%.

Let's go over this again, because this is super important.

With rent at 30% of your salary, you should be able to save 20% at the start of the month, have another 20% for all the most basic things in life, and 30% for some of the less basic but more enjoyable things in life. That still might not be a lot, but it's something, and you have a chance to save. With 20% saved, you can be free in your early 60s.

Too many people spend too much money living somewhere they "want" to live. That doesn't have to be a bad thing, if they already have 25X saved or that extra is coming out of the 30% they're spending on enjoyment. You could spend up to 60% on your apartment or house, as long as you recognise that you have no other enjoyment spending left over: no meals out, no holidays, no movies, no sports games. Not even a coffee in a coffee shop and definitely no avocado toast (or whatever today's popular special is!).

Alternative Living

More and more people are finding the typical way of life, of renting or buying a nice home in a nice area, too expensive and too constraining on the way they want to live, and so they opt for an alternative.

These range from campervans to boats to small houses to cabins in the woods. Don't dismiss these options. Even if they're not for you, they can perhaps inspire you to be creative about your own lifestyle. Search for alternative living on Facebook or Google to see how "the alternatives" live. It's really inspirational.

You don't get to spend money twice. If you try to do that, you'll keep going back into your savings. And that will mean you won't have any savings.

If you choose to spend 40% of your income on housing, because you really like a particular place and it works in other ways too, then please remember that you're going to have to budget only 20% for enjoyment spending now, not 30%.

It's possible to do better though. It's always possible. You can guarantee someone else is. The key here is to do research. Look around, and then look around again. Treat finding the best value accommodation in your town as a very important research project. Don't try to make it an attempt to show off your taste.

Property markets aren't efficient, which means that some people are charging too much and some others are charging less. If you buy or rent the first thing you see, or "fall in love" or "must have" something, then you will end up paying too much. If you do your research, you should be able to get that price back below 30% of your salary.

What if it's not possible to get a place to rent without paying more than 30%?

Then you really seriously have to reconsider the job that puts you in this position, and whether it's worth your time and energy. If you're doing a job that prevents you saving, you had better love it with every beat of your heart, because it isn't paying you enough to not love it.

And if you do love it with every beat of your heart … well, then there's your enjoyment, so you don't need any enjoyment spending and you can save that money instead. Accept that you have to live somewhere expensive to do a job you love, but you do love the job and it's all you need in life; then break down your salary as 20% saving, 50% rent, 30% other basic cost of living, because you're getting all the enjoyment, all the movies, all the restaurants, all the holidays, all the fun you need from doing this job you love.

It might be possible, but it sounds like a fairy tale to me. For everyone else living in the real world, 30% is all you should spend on rent!

2. Moving around

Rent is only one of the regular numbers going out of the door. There are a bunch of other "utilities" that just can't be avoided. Electricity, water, travel to work, basic food – enough to survive. All these have to be included in the 50% total. They have to be included there, because they are as important to living as basic shelter, and also because they're kind of attached already.

For example, the cost of travelling to work will be very closely related to where you choose to live. It may be too expensive to live across the road from your job, and so you live further out with higher travel costs.

However, those travel costs may, at times and in some places, be even higher than the difference in rent you would pay, so you have to balance the two things out. "Rent plus travel costs" becomes your equation, and if it's a long trip to work, you should factor in travel time too, so "rent plus travel cost plus travel time" should be how you judge an apartment.

You really need to research this. In some towns, everyone wants to live right in the middle of town, so the rent there becomes very expensive. Then you need to look at two things: what are my commuting options, or can I get a better job that's not in such a central area? Sometimes the commuting options are pretty cheap and effective, and so you can just commute from a nice place out of town and work that way.

In some other towns, everyone wants to live out of town, and so the commute is really awful and actually there can be bargains right in the middle of town.

In other places, you can sometimes find ways of commuting that are actually fun and that you enjoy, and that gets added into the whole bargain.

(If you really, really want to save money and enjoy more of your life, you could try to walk, run or bike to work. So many people rent a house, buy a car, pay for a gym membership – and then run on a treadmill after work. And then they complain that they don't have any time to exercise, they aren't getting any fitter and don't have any savings. Think. Research. Do things differently and you can change your life for the better.)

If you can't get what you want by doing what you're doing, looking where you're looking or working where you're working, don't be afraid to totally change it up. Look at something different. Different job, different town, different country.

In the end, this is one thing that really rewards your research. People spend way too much time "looking at apartments" to get a place they think will be a dream home, because it has a nice kitchen, or whatever, and not enough time researching the economics of transport and locality. This should be the main if not the only thing that determines where you rent.

3. Survival Food

So your commute is one essential extra component you have to add into your basic living costs. Then there are the other obvious things: electricity, heating, basic communications (phone, Internet, etc.) that you're going to have to pay for wherever you live. All these go into your 50%.

I include basic food in here because I think you should split your food choices: survive and enjoy. If you don't split your food choices, the temptation becomes too great to think that you have to "enjoy" every single meal, that every meal becomes a treat, and then you start buying individual meals, eating from takeaways and in restaurants and, once again, you've spent your 30% on enjoyment before you've had any real enjoyment.

Buy food in bulk that you like to eat and that stores well. There are hundreds of examples of this. Rice. Dried beans. Pasta. Noodles. Canned products. All of these things can be bought for the whole month, or even for a few months, at one go, normally at much cheaper prices than if you buy one at a time. They can all be stored for a long time, and they can all be prepared in lots of different ways.

Find the place that sells these things at the best prices in bulk and calculate the best way of buying them. Don't buy one can at a time. Find a place that will sell you a box of 24 for the price of 12 individual tins. That's 12 free meals. Noodles in big packs cost less than half the price of individual packs – for exactly the same thing. Big bags of dried beans can sometimes cost the price of just one or two cans, but contain 20 times the amount of beans.

This forms the background of keeping you alive. Remember, that's what this 50% is for. It's your "cost of basic living."

I know it doesn't sound much fun, but it's not supposed to. This is supposed to enable you to keep 30% for your fun spending.

When I was in college in London, I shared a house with other students – all trying to live on a government grant in one of the world's most expensive cities. Compared to today's students, we were incredibly lucky that we got those grants and that we didn't have to borrow to pay our fees, but the immediate spending choices were just as tough, so we used to take some extreme measures.

We had to: the cheapest rent in the whole of London was nowhere near 30% of our income, it was more like 75%, so we all had to get jobs to survive as well as borrowing money – but we also got creative with our food.

We would all get our money at the beginning of term and pay our rent for three months at one go. As this left us with almost no money, we would then scour London's markets and warehouses for the cheapest food we could find that would last. Sometimes this would be boxes of tins where the labels had fallen off, so every meal was a surprise. The debate over whether a tin contained beef stew or dog food would often take ten times longer than the meal itself (because you would eat it very quickly, just in case!).

Sometimes it was better to buy packages of food that we didn't particularly like, because, by the end of term when we really had no money, and therefore nothing to eat, we would still have that. When the last few coins finally ran out, that's when we hit the bargain boxes and still had enough to get through.

The idea was the same though. We were buying survival food so that when our money ran out, we would have food left – to survive!

30% Fun?

I'm sure you've been looking forward to this part, the part where you can have some fun .... I'm sorry to break it to you, but I've got bad news and worse news for you.

The bad news is that this is the area where you need to exercise the most control.

Controlled fun? Yes, because this is the place where it's easiest to over-spend, and easiest to totally de-rail your budgeting and your saving. If you don't control your fun spending, it will wreck everything else.

The even worse news is that you may find you have to save some of this fun money too. Yes, sorry, but if you want to go on a holiday, and you need to save for that, you can't take that saving out of your emergency fund, or your freedom fund. The clues are in the names!

If you want to save up for a holiday, you will have to create a separate holiday fund, in a different envelope from your savings and spending money. It will also give you a chance to see how much of your future that holiday is costing you – if it costs you a year of your real saving, it is pushing your freedom back a year!

If you want to redecorate your apartment, buy a more expensive TV or phone or tablet or whatever you kids are using these days, and you need to "save" for it, that saving isn't being done in your 20%. That saving isn't saving for spending. If you want to save for those things, it has to come from your fun money.

Can I At Least Have Some Fun Spending Money?

You don't need any advice on how to have fun. Who does? It's easy. Just do what you enjoy.

Does that mean cutting back on the amount you spend needs to be dull? Not at all, and particularly not if you learn to treat it as a bit of a game, with these two top techniques from the financial industry: arbitrage and negotiation.

The Fun Arbitrage

Arbitrage is a term used in finance that means you can buy exactly the same thing cheaper in one place than you can in another. In finance, you would then ideally sell it back and keep the profit. In your fun spending, you can use arbitrage to find the thing you really want at a much, much cheaper price.

Like what? If you really need to treat someone to a meal at a fancy restaurant, then go at lunch. Fancy restaurants are always much cheaper at lunch time, and you're less likely to order alcohol, which cuts the bill as well and makes it less likely that you order the crazy expensive stuff, which further cuts the bill. If you do your research, you may find that a super-famous restaurant that can cost FN100 or FN200 per head at night may cost FN20 at lunch. You just saved 80–90%.

Now save it!

And you know what? Cheap restaurants are often just as cheap at night as they are at lunchtime, so go to cheap restaurants at night-time, expensive ones for lunch. It's the same food and the same chef and the same room. Just different time and different price.

Arbitrage shouldn't exist, because the same thing should always be the same price, but there's often a good reason why different prices exist.

For example, a lot of people like to go to smart restaurants for a special occasion, and they like to do that at night – so the restaurants can charge more. The restaurants are already paying their rent for the whole day, so they might as well open at lunch and offer a slightly limited service for a much lower price, but the extra money helps them cover their costs. There's your arbitrage opportunity.

Whenever you can, look for an arbitrage; and if it offers something you like, then try to take advantage.

Other examples?

Go on holiday when other people aren't. Want to go to a place where people go at the weekend? Find out what the rates are like mid-week. If it's a financial or business area, weekends may actually be cheaper, so try that instead. People only go during school holidays? Go at other times.

There are lots of other cheaper examples. I often buy the fresh food in a supermarket that is priced down to sell late in the day. It reminds me that I need to eat it sooner rather than later, and it will be ready to eat (not that typical supermarket un-ripe un-readiness), and I feel I'm doing the environment and the supermarket a favour by reducing their wastage.

A lot of success in saving isn't avoiding doing the things you want to do, but finding ways of doing those things at a better price. It's very rare that the better price doesn't exist – you just need to look hard enough. If there's a bakery near you that discounts its pastries in the evening, try to walk past it on your way home, for example, when you need some fresh bread, saving money on your bread and your commute.

After you do this successfully a couple of times, you'll probably start to enjoy it. Arbitraging can actually become fun in itself, making you feel clever, getting ahead of the system. Finding how to get the same thing you really wanted for a lot less can actually become a way of having fun.

Just make sure it doesn't affect what you spend your money on. You don't want to buy something you didn't actually want just because it's suppos- edly a bargain. That's still a waste of money. Just pay less for the things you do want and find new ways of doing this.

The Fun Negotiation

The other way to find stuff for less money is to negoti- ate. Ask for money off. Ask again. And then ask again.

You can ask for some money off whenever you think you can and see how far you can go. Don't do this on the bus, because the people behind you will be annoyed and it won't work, but you'll find lots of other places where you can get a little bit of a discount just by asking.

Think about it: a 10% discount on everything you ever do is an immediate extra 10% saving rate, and maybe 10 years of freedom. Just by negotiating.

You will save more money if you have a system to negotiate, and it starts in a similar way to the fun arbi- trage: with research, because you have to know what the prices are at different places and at different times.

Sweating The Big Stuff

You should do this on all big spending. Whenever you can, you should see if there's a way you can get more than two suppliers to fight to give you their services cheaper. You see how that sounds? It doesn't sound possible, but it's just a question of asking.

You should really do this with houses, whether buying or renting. So many people think the purpose of house-hunting is to find the house they really like, just to prove they have taste, but all they have achieved by that is reducing their negotiation position. Find five you really like, and then make them all bids 20% below what they're asking. See who takes the lowest amount.

Isn't this all a bit like hard work? Well, it would be if you visited them all, but you can test out the water before you see them, making it easier, telling them it may be a bit expensive for you and asking if they are flexible on pricing. If they say no, they're less likely to cut the price and so you might not want to see that one.

This is the way my wife negotiated lower rent everywhere we lived that is probably worth a quarter of our savings today. If she hadn't done that every year, finding savings elsewhere would have been much harder.

She deliberately found a few houses she was happy to live in and then let them fight for the best offer. Sometimes there was one she preferred a little, but a second one would hit her with such a big discount that she would take that. Other times, the favourite one was the best deal. Most of the time we just stayed where we were, but not just paying what the landlord first asked. He knew we were prepared to leave, because we knew too, and then he cut the price to let us stay.

You should do it with cars. If you're buying secondhand (in most countries, you should always buy secondhand, as the showroom and salesman cost you 20 to 30% of the price), then you can scout out four or five cars you like the look of and try to bid them all down. See if any take your bid. See if they sound like they might.

As with arbitrage, you can also make this part of your fun – seeing how much cheaper than the original price you can get, how much less you can pay than people who don't negotiate. You can make it a point of pride, how much you managed to negotiate off the price of your big-ticket items – and put into the bank.

Remember, something you like about that hotel or house or car today might not be such a big deal later, and you may eventually prefer the cheaper one ... and yet have a much better, more secure life as a result of finding the arbitrage and then negotiating to make it bigger.

Example: Negotiate A Holiday

Holidays are big-ticket items for all of us, probably the biggest after housing, and as such they're best avoided! If you can't avoid them, though, they're best "negotiated."

When you're planning one, don't fool yourself into thinking that you can do research to find out which is the best place to stay, because you can't really know.

Tripadvisor doesn't really help, because reviews are always subjective, and the hotel websites are obviously all just marketing. If you spend time studying to find out which one you think is the best, you're actually just playing into the hands of their marketing departments. That's what they want you to do.

Instead, research how many hotels are up to your acceptable standard and then email all of them directly for their best price.

Just because you aren't using one of the booking systems, you should already get a decent discount, and if you've asked enough, one of them should cut you a pretty good deal. You could then stay in the one that gave you the lowest answer, and you've already saved some money.

Not bad ... but we haven't started negotiating yet. That's just asking for a discount, not negotiating.

Don't you think it would be fairer to tell the other hotels that you've got an offer that low and, unless they can make theirs cheaper, you will take that offer?

Maybe they will. Then you can use that price as your starting point, and see if the original one will make it cheaper again, or give you a free buffet breakfast (buffet breakfasts should always be free – the hotel has already prepared all that food and hired the staff, so you make no difference).

You can only do this if you do your research properly and have a selection of hotels you don't mind staying in. If you've studied lots of pictures and decided that you think one of them is much nicer than the rest, then they've won and you've lost.

By research, I mean working out how many places there are that you wouldn't mind staying at, places that feel roughly the same to you, from their online reviews and pictures, and that you suspect might all be a lot of fun.

Let's face it: lots of hotels are actually really, really nice. You shouldn't make your own life harder by trying to choose without really knowing – let the hotels make it easier for you by getting them to cut their prices!

Discomfort Training

If the thought of asking for discounts or negotiating makes you uncomfortable, remember that doing new things is often uncomfortable. Doing things other people aren't doing – whether it's refusing to spend, saving up your money, negotiating for discounts – is uncomfortable.

Your life won't change unless you're prepared to be a little uncomfortable occasionally.

Whenever you hear yourself thinking "I can't do that," that's your comfort level telling you it doesn't want to do it, whatever it is: running a marathon, raising money for charity, singing on stage, public speaking, saving money, negotiating for a bigger discount.

Of course you can do it; it's just making you uncomfortable.

But discomfort is worth getting used to. Unless you're uncomfortable, you could be doing more, whether it's exercising, saving or negotiating.

Discomfort is the key. You need to be prepared for discomfort.

So go out now and get a discount. Right now, ask for a discount on the next thing you buy. A coffee. A meal. A house. Ask for 10% off.

Don't pretend like it's a joke. Don't tell them a fairy tale book told you to do it. Just ask. If you get it, you just saved 10%. If you don't get it, you survived, and you got stronger.

Tim Ferriss, the author of all the *Four Hour* books, lists out a number of ways of training for discomfort, but asking for a discount is in many ways the most useful one for our purposes. It will make you stronger and it will save you money.

Free (Cool) Movements That Discourage Spending

If you're still a bit uncomfortable cutting back on your spending, worried that people might think you are cheap, then take a look at the following groups:

- minimalists
- mindfulness

- environmentalists

- frugalists

- charities

- stoics.

At some point in the trend cycle, it's cool to be one of the above or work with them. Personally, I think all of them are cool, all of the time, but that's just me, probably over-using the word "cool" like no young person would.

One thing that is genuinely cool about all of them, though, is that they all discourage a way of life that involves spending too much money.

I know some of the people who promote them do so for money, so they might tell you that you need a book to tell you how to be properly minimalist, or buy different (more expensive) detergent to be really environmental, but don't listen to them.

The key to being minimal is to own and use less, and the way to do that is to buy less. That saves you money.

The key to being environmental is to limit the damage you do to the planet, and the best way to do that is to buy less. You can use cheap secondhand things, cheap recycled things, not expensive things that are recyclable (but won't be recycled).

The key to charities is to help other people, and by seeing how tough some other people's lives are, your need to buy things will generally reduce.

The simple key to mindfulness is becoming more aware of the things you do without thinking, like spending.

The key to being frugal is pretty obvious.

The real beauty of these movements is that they provide things like a support network and a philosophy behind reducing your spending. If you join one, you won't be cutting your spending to be cheap, or look boring because you're saving: you'll be part of a trendy movement. You'll be saving the planet. You'll learn from super-cool movement leaders how you can get more life with less money and have a greater impact with less money.

You won't be going without. You'll be getting more, but spending less to do that ... and saving more too.

Should I Be Worried About My Spending?

What You Don't Monitor, You Can't Save

How do you know how much you spend on stuff? Well, if you have no money left over at the end of the month, so you're spending everything you earn … that's one way of knowing. A bad way!

It's much better to know exactly what you're spending on everything you buy, so you can really know if you're spending well or if you could spend less on particular things. That would be better, right? Then you could really budget.

How far are you right now from saving 20%, spending 30% on rent or accommodation, 20% on other basics and 30% on fun stuff? The only way you'll find out how close you are to that is to monitor your spending closely. In the past, that would have required constant attention to your spending, as well as some kind of complicated system for recording and comparing notes.

And you can still do that. Pop a little notebook in your pocket and record everything you spend. At the end of the month, check how much you've spent in that notebook, take that number away from your income, and see if the resulting number matches how much you've got left in your account. If it doesn't, you've been spending without recording.

That's the old way – and sometimes it can be nice to do things that way. The effort of writing down every spend will help us notice what we're spending on more intensely. If you don't have time when you're in the shop, slip the receipt into the notebook. If you forget stuff during the day, do a catch-up later on.

If you're one of those people that think it all sounds a bit old-fashioned, then you can probably find an app that will make it easier: one that will auto-record some purchases. You can even take photos of your receipts to record later on, and the app will present everything for you at the end of the month. Pretty little charts showing you where you are spending most – and where you could cut back.

Whichever system sounds right for you. Find one that works, that you like using, and record your spending for a while. You are bound to find out something that surprises you, and that could be an extra way for you to save some money – or even re-focus your spending on to things that actually give you more pleasure.

If you don't monitor it, you won't know; and if you don't know, you can't change.

In *The Thousand Dollar Journal*, we created sheets to track our saving and spending, analyse that spending, and set a budget for the following week. We think people who don't track their spending, underestimate what they spend money on by about 25%. That's enough savings to set you free at 56, right there.

There are some samples of those sheets in a couple of pages, and you can get free versions on www.sevendollarmillionaire.com and remember our "Start Here" page. We will update that with the latest and greatest budgeting apps we can find: www.sevendollarmillionaire.com/start-here.

The First Seven Cuts

We all have some things we spend money on that we know we shouldn't. Some are just regular habits that we could stop if we tried; others are really bad habits that we know we should try to stop right away. Although individually the savings might seem small, they add up to a lot of money in lost savings and investments.

1. **Cigarettes?** The average amount of money spent per adult on cigarettes per year in the US is $337, almost a dollar a day. In the UK, the average spend per household per day is about 50p or GBP175 a year.

2. **Alcohol?** Americans also spend more than a dollar a day on alcohol. Brits spend about a pound per day on booze.

3. **Eating out?** This is a surprisingly big one: on average, Americans spend more than $8 a day eating out. If they cut that in half – and added it to their $2 of savings from cigarettes and alcohol – they'd have $6 saved. British households spend an average of GBP45 a week eating out. It shouldn't be impossible to cut that in half and save GBP21 a week, or GBP3 a day.

4. **Other drinks?** Americans spend $2.50 on soft drinks and bottled water (mainly on soft drinks). Brits spend a bit less than a pound.

5. **Cable and Satellite TV** services in the US cost the average subscriber more than $3 a day.

6. And keeping a **landline** service in your house, when you only really use your mobile, could be costing you $1 a day.

7. And of course, when talking about daily costs
we could cut, we can't ignore our **café latte**.
Let's say that costs $3 where you are, and you
could take it from home for next to nothing.

Altogether, the average American could save $20
a day by cutting back all these items, and $10 by
halving them.

If you save $20 a day and invest it for 7% returns,
it becomes a million dollars in just 35 years, and just
$10 a day turns into a million in 45 years. That's what
spending on those seven items costs the average
American in their lifetime: a million dollars.

And the same numbers work for pounds, rupees or
even FNs. Cut those seven items, and *Happy Ever After*
will get a lot closer.

The Craziest Spending Of All

The American self-storage industry generated $36 billion
of revenue in 2017 – that's a bit over $110 per person
in the US, or $300 per household. As only about 9% of
households actually do rent, however, they are averaging
more than $3,000 per year on renting storage space.

That's more than the minimum amount of money
that people need to save every year to become a millionaire in a 50-year working career.

We should spell that out. The amount of money
that almost a tenth of all households in the USA spend
on storage could, if saved and invested, turn into a million dollars in their lifetimes.

And let's be clear here: we're not just talking
about the money being wasted on storage here. This is
money being wasted storing the stuff that money was
wasted on in the first place. Who knows how quickly
those people could have become millionaires if they
had saved the money on the things in the storage, as
well as the rental for the storage.

Our Fourth Step Out Of The Woods

In the previous stages of our M.I.S.S.I.O.N., we began to understand what the woods are – and how we get out of them. Rather than spend our whole lives lost, we know that it is possible to cut our working career down to 28 years by saving 35% of our income. That would mean we can be out of the woods before 50, as in the diagram below.

But it could be better. If we could find areas of our spending where we could cut back just a little, where we feel we're wasting money, we could save faster. Could we save 45%?

If we could save 45%, that could be our forest. We could be out of the woods after only 22 years of work, not long after 40 years old – living the rest of our life, however long that is, on the money that our savings and investing is making for us.

Earning a little more money helped us get from 15% to 25%, and learning how to save in a more systematic way could probably helped us get from 25% to

35%; but if we're going to get to 45%, we will need to change the way we think about the money we spend. We might need a total lifestyle change.

But look at how much closer to the edge of the woods it just got us. That's better than whatever it was we were just thinking of buying, surely?

Free Stuff: *Thousand Dollar Journal* Budget Sheets

MY FIRST WEEK'S SPENDING

STARTING SUNDAY
__ / __ / __
(Write Sunday's date here)

Categories/Types:
- Meals (Food, Snacks, Drinks)
- Utilities (Transport, Phone)
- Beauty & Health (Make-up, Clothing, Toiletries, Medicine)
- Entertainment (Karaoke, Movies/Concerts, Picnic/Party)
- Gifts · Family/Charity · Others (You choose.)

Track your spending as you go through the week on the table below.

NO.	DAY	DESCRIPTION		AMOUNT SPENT	CATEGORY/TYPE
eg	Sunday	Sandwich (Make my own next time to save money)	NEED/WANT	$2.50	Snacks
			NEED/WANT		
			NEED/WANT		
			NEED/WANT		
			NEED/WANT		
			NEED/WANT		
			NEED/WANT		
			NEED/WANT		
			NEED/WANT		
			NEED/WANT		
			NEED/WANT		
			NEED/WANT		
			NEED/WANT		
			NEED/WANT		
			NEED/WANT		

⚠ If this is not enough space, STOP SPENDING! | TOTAL

★ For everything you buy, circle whether you really needed it or just wanted it at that time. This is important!

Figure 5.1

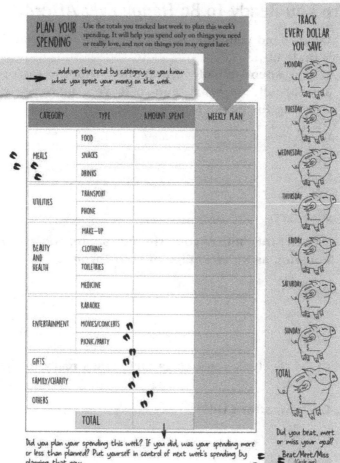

Figure 5.2

Are You Ready To Be *Happy Ever After?*

Did you spend your time paying attention in that stage? Let's find out ...

1. **If you spend all of your money without saving any at all, at what age will you be free of working for money?**

    a) 45.

    b) 55.

    c) 65.

    d) Never.

2. **What's the most you should spend on your housing, as a percentage of your income?**

    a) 30%.

    b) 40%.

    c) 50%.

    d) As much as you like as long as it's really, really nice.

3. **Can you afford this?**

    a) No.

    b) Yes.

    c) Not if you're asking yourself that question.

4. **If you are researching a purchase on the Internet (or in the real world), what are you NOT looking for?**

    a) The best price.

    b) A selection of options that you wouldn't mind buying, so that you can then start to negotiate the sellers down to lower prices.

c) One with the best website and the prettiest pictures because it must be the best, even if it is more expensive.

5. **How often do you spend on "once in a lifetime" things?**

   a) Never.

   b) Once.

   c) Once you have spent on one "once in a lifetime" thing, you feel tempted to do it again.

6. **Does asking for a 10% discount make you feel uncomfortable?**

   a) No. (So why don't you do it more often?)

   b) Some of the time. (You need to do it more often!)

   c) Yes. (You really need to do it more often, so you become comfortable with buying things for less. There is no shame in it.)

7. **Can you take money for a holiday, or a party, or something else fun from your regular savings account?**

   a) No.

   b) No.

   c) You have to save for this separately!

Answers

1. d) If you spend everything and save nothing, you will never be free. This isn't a fairy tale, princess.
2. a) 30%.
3. c)

4. c) You are looking for the best price among the things you don't mind. Looking for the nicest resort is wasting your time researching the work of the marketing departments.
5. a) Try not to think that. It becomes a habit.
6. Do it all the time!
7. All of the above.

Free (Reducing) Spending Stuff: Geo-arbitrage

Geo-arbitrage is a long word for a simple and really useful thing; something everyone should think about and use on their path to financial freedom. It just means that some places are cheaper than others, and we can use that to our advantage.

Here are just a couple of quick ways …

We need 25X our spending to achieve our Freedom Formula, but it isn't necessarily 25X our spending where we live today. If you can live somewhere else much (MUCH) cheaper, then it could be 25X that amount. There are places all over the world where renting a nice apartment is only a few hundred dollars a month and food costs a couple of dollars a day. If you could live by a tropical beach all year long for less than $5,000, then your Freedom Formula could be $125,000.

If you really don't want to live on a tropical beach like that, you could add a couple of thousand dollars a year to your costs and travel between different tropical beaches, or cheap cities around the world.

Or you could travel for a few months a year at those kinds of prices, going off-peak to avoid the crowds and high prices, all the while spicing up your life and keeping your costs down.

On her website www.birdsofafire.com, financial independence guru Olivia lists out the best cities in the world to use for geo-arbitrage, along with tons of other great advice for FIRE enthusiasts.

"Magic beans? Are they even a thing?"

Jack And The Giant
Bean Stock

(Or How Jack Slayed The Corporate Beast And Made Massive Returns.)

Charlie the talking frog realised that the princess was never going to learn about real life by looking out of the window of an enchanted castle.

"You need to change into something less princess-y, so we can go outside," he told the princess.

"But I don't have anything less princess-y," she complained. "Why would I? I'm a princess."

"Ok. Don't worry, I'll magic something up."

The princess was so disappointed. She was past the point of expecting a pumpkin to be turned into a carriage, but when Charlie had mentioned "magic" she hadn't imagined it would involve borrowing some of her dad's old clothes and being pushed into a puddle.

"You're too clean," Charlie had laughed.

"That really isn't much of an apology," the princess said. "And I've never thought being too clean could be a problem before."

At that moment, a sad-looking boy arrived at the puddle with an even sadder-looking cow. "I don't suppose you want to buy my cow, do you? No, you look too clean to buy a cow. I'd better do as my mum asked, and take him to the market," and he continued along the path.

"Who's that?" asked the princess.

"That's Jack," explained Charlie. "He's just called 'Simple Jack' at the moment, but in a short time he'll be world-famous as 'Jack The Giant Killer'."

"Oh no! Is he dangerous? Did my father ask him to kill a giant to win my hand in marriage?" asked the princess.

"No. His mother has sent him to market to sell the family cow, but no one wants to buy it, so he eventually accepts some magic beans for the cow."

"'Magic beans'?" asked the princess. "Are they even a thing?"

"Of course they're not," grunted Charlie, "but Jack didn't know they were a scam, and nor did anyone else. When Jack got home with neither the cow nor any money, his mother was furious and just threw the beans out of the window. When he woke up ..."

"I know this! The beans had grown into a huge beanstalk, reaching right up into the clouds, where a giant lived, who Jack killed and stole his treasure, a sack of gold coins? I'm sure I heard that story somewhere before ..." the princess mumbled as she began to realise how silly the whole story sounded.

"Well, that's fair, you might have, because Jack told that story," Charlie explained. "He woke up the next morning to find a huge beanstalk, with beans growing all over it, enough that he and his mum could eat that day, and with enough left over for the next day."

"So no giant?" asked the princess.

"Not yet. It turned out that the beans weren't edible. He got sick and his mum got really sick, so sick she *almost died. This made Jack furious, and he chased down the man who sold him the magic beans, who was really sorry, and told him which company had sold him the magic beans, Giant Agricultural Corporation."*

"Oh … that kind of giant," said the princess, less impressed.

"Jack sued the company for a sack of gold coins, and then used the money to form an activist investment fund that fought other giant corporations that treated people badly, and made a lot of money in the process," Charlie explained.

"And the story about the beanstalk and the real giant?" the princess asked.

"That was just a fairy tale, princess. Jack made enough money from his corporate giant-killing that he never had to work again, but he didn't want people to know that, so he made up the fairy tale about the beanstalk to keep people away."

"He made enough money that he never had to work again? How much is that, Charlie?"

"Finally," Charlie gurgled. "You're asking the right kind of question."

The Chapter 6 Cheat Sheet

How We Make Money Work For Us

1. Investing is how we get money to work for us instead of us working for money. Done well, this should be how we make most of the money we need in our lives!

2. The magic of compound returns is how money grows faster and faster – and the earlier you start, the better the magic works. Start now.

3. We need to understand what risk is – and then take some. Thinking we're taking no risk by doing nothing is more dangerous to our future freedom than doing something risky.

4. We should be compensated for taking Risk by Returns – the profit on our investments. More returns will mean more risk, but we can reduce that by Integrating our risks with our lives, Spreading them over different assets, and Knowing what we are doing: R-RISK!

5. Learn how to avoid scams. Start by not trusting anyone. Don't trust people who tell you to trust them. Don't trust guarantees. Ask as many

questions as you want, and don't trust people who can't or won't answer them.

6. Investing is a lifetime of learning. Don't worry that you haven't learnt it all, because no one has, and no one can. Learn a little and start from there. If you can enjoy it, that will help, so try to find an investment area you find a little interesting.

7. The most famous investor ever said we should all invest 90% of our money in a cheap index fund. His will stipulates that his executors should do the same for his family when he dies. This should be our goal, at least.

CHAPTER 6

I For Investing

One of the reasons lots of people under-invest is because they don't really understand it. And one of the reasons they don't understand it is because a lot of the people who do understand it over-complicate it. Sometimes they do that so they can keep other people out of a job, and sometimes they do it to make simple stuff look clever.

We're not going to do that. We want to keep it simple here, because we don't need to do anything complex to invest well. We can make good money by keeping it simple, as long as we understand why we're doing it.

If there has ever been a true wizard of the investing world, it's Warren Buffett, and things don't get much simpler than his advice for beginning investors: put 10% of your assets into treasury bonds and 90% into an index fund, preferably one with low fees that tracks the S&P500 (for American investors).

"Who's Warren Buffet?" the princess asked.

"He's like a kindly old wizard ..." Charlie explained.

"Oooh, let's go see him!" the princess interrupted.

"Well we could go to Omaha in May, when he meets people, but there will be thousands of other people there and anyway, he wrote down all of his magic spells for making money every year."

"Oh, he makes money ..." the princess sighed. "I thought he might turn you into a prince."

The goal of investing is to make sure that when we want to spend our savings, we get at least as much time and energy as we put in. We don't want our time and energy to go down in value. We want it to go up. Ideally, we want to take out more time and energy than we put in. That way, money works for us, rather than the other way around.

Yes, money can make more money for us than we ever put in. Invested well – and early – most of the money we need in life can actually come from our investments, not from our hard work.

We can buy things that increase in value over time. We can then take those things, sell them, and buy things that haven't increased in value as much – and that way, we get more time and energy back for our money. If we don't do it, the things we want to buy are likely to increase in price over time, the value of our money will go down through time, and we'll only be able to buy less time and energy with them.

"You said we were going to learn about the magic of investing," the princess complained to Charlie.

"We're about to learn some magic right now," said Charlie. "Let's take a quick break and learn about the magic of compounding."

"Compounding?" said the princess. "That sounds like we might need a cauldron."

"No. We just need a calculator," said Charlie.

"Oh."

Magic Trick 1: Doubling your money with the "Rule of 72"

One of the best things about investing is that, done well, it benefits from the (almost) magical effect of compounding. I say "almost" because although there's no such thing as magic, compounding can feel like it.

One of the oldest fairy tales in the world features the magic of compounding. The story tells of an ancient emperor being so impressed by the newly invented game of chess that he rewarded the inventor by telling him he could have anything he wants. The inventor was obviously very clever (he invented chess, after all) and so asked for rice to be placed on the chessboard, one grain on the first square, two on the second, four on the third, and so on, doubling the amount on every subsequent square.

The emperor agreed – thinking that a few grains of rice was very cheap – but before his servants had got anywhere near putting rice on the last square, he had no rice left and owed his whole nation to the inventor of the game, because he didn't know how quickly compounding creates huge numbers.

That's the magic of compounding, which is how investments grow faster, as returns increase every year by the amount of gains they have made before and so start to grow faster and faster.

Looked at over a longer time frame it is, according to a famous quote, "the most powerful force in the universe". It is how investing early in life can bring huge rewards later, as our funds double, double and double again.

Our funds don't need to be invested amazingly well for this to happen. If your savings can double every 10 years (which needs a 7.2% return), they will become 32 times larger in 50 years: FN1,000 becomes FN32,000 in 50 years, and FN10,000 becomes FN320,000.

It's true for dollars, pounds and rupees too: just one of them can make another 31 in 50 years, without amazing investing.

Think of that every time you want to buy something rather than invest: work out if you would pay 32X more for it, because that's what it will cost you in lost investment earnings.

It's important to understand how quickly different return rates double.

- If Jill invests FN100 in something that returns 25% a year, most people would think it will take four years to double to FN200.

  - 100 plus 25 plus 25 plus 25 plus 25 equals 200; but that's wrong.

- Jill would actually double her money in just over three years.

  - The numbers above were right, but only for year 1. 100 plus 25.

  - In year 2, Jill will get a 25% return on FN125, not FN100, which is a little over FN31.

  - That means that at the start of year 3, she will have FN156, and 25% of that is FN40.

  - So in 3 years she will have gone from FN100 to FN196.

That's the magic of compounding.

The numbers are a little easier using a 10% return and, let's face it, from an investing standpoint that's more realistic than expecting 25% every year: 10% doesn't double in 10 years, but in a little over 7.

This is where the "Rule of 72" comes in: 72 is the number of years it takes for a 1% return to double. Not 100 years, as you might think if you did the equation "100 plus one plus one plus one plus ...," but just 72.

Magically, if you divide 72 by your return, you get the rough number of years it will take for that return double. So 2% returns double in 36 years, 5% in 14 years, 10% in 7 years, and 25% in about 3 years.

The rule of 72 is an easy way of calculating how quickly your money will double. It's also a good way of seeing the benefits of taking extra risk. The benefit of aiming for a 10% return, compared to a 5% return, is that your money will almost double in 7 years; while 5% returns will take 15 years to reach that total. In 50 years, 10% returns double 7 times; while 5% returns double a little over 3 times. In 50 years, $7 invested for 5% returns becomes just $80, while $7 invested for 10% for 50 years becomes more than $800. Ten times more money, for 5% difference!

The Long-Term Magic Of Compounding

The magic of compounding is also the best reason to start investing early. The first few years of compounding might not look that impressive, but later years start to show huge gains.

- If Jill invested FN1,000 in investments with a 10% return when she was 21 years old, at 42 years old those will be worth FN8,000. The FN1,000 will have made FN7,000 all on its own.

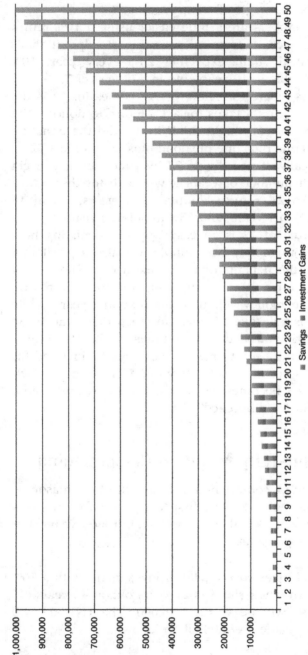

Figure 6.1

- By the time she is 56 it will have quadrupled again to FN32,000.

- At 63, it will be worth FN64,000. In just the 7 years between 56 and 63 years old, that original FN1,000 will increase in value by FN32,000.

- If instead Jack waits until 28 to invest FN1,000, between 56 and 63 it will increase by FN16,000. If he waits until 35, it will increase by just FN8,000.

That's why it's best to start early. Compounding's magic is much stronger if it starts early. Let's look at another version of the *Seven Dollar Millionaire* chart (In Figure 6.1):

If we save $7 a day, $50 every week, and invest it for a 7% return, it will become a million dollars in 50 years. But in 40 years, it will only have become $500,000, and in 20 it will be just over $100,000. The earlier you start compounding, the better.

This is how our money makes more money for us than we ever need to earn by working in our lives – and we don't even need to be investing wizards like Warren Buffett to achieve that.

So, what stops everyone from doing this? The fact that they haven't been told it can happen – and instead they're told it's risky!

Zoinks! What's R-RISK?

"R-RISK" is not only how Scooby Doo might pronounce risk, it spells out 5 different concepts that will help us understand investing properly and overcome one of the main things that stops people making their money work for them – being scared of taking risks.

R–R is for Risk–Return. First, we need to understand the nature of risk: that everything is a risk. Every choice we make in life involves a risk that another good choice might be better, but the risk we take should always have some benefits attached – return.

The key to investing is to try to reduce your risk while getting the benefit of investing – higher returns. We're going to look at three ways of doing this.

I is for Integrate. While risk is unavoidable, there are risks you don't need to take, and you can reduce your risk by aligning your investing with who you are: where you live, how you live, how old you are, what you want from life and when you want your money back. The more we integrate the risks we take with the way we want to live our lives, the further we reduce the risk of making mistakes we don't need to make.

S is for Spreading that investment around into different things, so if one goes down in value, the others may go up. This is known in finance as diversification – and is also known as the only free lunch in finance. That's good, but it can be fun too.

K is for Knowledge, because you need to know at least a little to do this. This stage will get you started on that, and the more you learn, the less risk you will be taking – so be prepared to keep on learning, reducing your risk and increasing your return.

So how do you invest? You have to take risk.

R for Risk

One of the things that stops most people from investing is that they think it is too risky, but it's important to understand that everything has some risk, every choice involves risking that the other choice is better.

Even choosing not to do anything – the sadly all-too-common "do nothing" strategy – involves the risk that doing something, anything, would have been better than doing nothing at all.

Or is riskiness stopping you from investing in anything more complicated than a savings account, or whatever you think is the "safest" investment for your money? When in reality, a combination of different "riskier" investments can be much safer than just one thing that looks like the safest investment.

In The Future ...

What risk really means is that none of us can predict the future. Really. No one can predict the future. Not you, not the person paid to make up the horoscope in the newspaper, not a hedge fund manager talking on TV like he knows everything about everything, nor even a 95-year-old Bulgarian widow who predicted the end of the world 20 years ago by talking in crazy verses.

We have to have expectations about the future all the time though. Every time we sit on a chair, we expect it not to break. We walk to the bus stop in expectation that a bus will come along.

In some places, with a really efficient bus system, you'll expect that bus to come along at a precise time. In countries with less reliable bus systems, you will expect to stand at the bus stop a bit longer, hoping that a bus comes along soon. It might. But it might come along a lot later (and then, of course, three will come!).

You might think that's an expectation, not a "prediction", but it's a good comparison because it shows that your expectation about the future can be more or less reliable in different circumstances. Chairs don't often break when you sit on them. Buses sometimes come when you expect them. And just like going to a bus stop, or preparing to sit on a chair, we have to predict the future because the future is going to happen.

When we invest, we are also trying to predict the future, because we expect to get our money back in the future with a particular "return" (the second R is coming up in a minute) that will enable us to convert that money into (hopefully) more time and energy than we put in to get it. We are trying to predict the future.

The fact that the investment return is further away in time than either the chair or the bus stop is what makes it harder to predict. And some investments are similarly hard or easy to predict. Let's walk through a simple example ...

Jack And Jill Went Up The Bank

Putting your money into a bank deposit is often seen as one of the lowest risk things you can do, as the bank will give you your money back later, with almost no risk to that outcome. It should give you back exactly the amount you put in, plus interest, unless the bank goes broke – and even then in some countries the government will save the bank and make sure you get your money back.

So, if Jack put FN100 in his bank account, he is very likely to get FN100 back. It is very unlikely he will get FN110 or FN90, or zero. Probably a million times out of a million, he will get FN100 back – almost like sitting in a chair. This is very low risk; although with no return, it is also not a great investment. Over time, as inflation pushes up the prices of things he wants to buy, it will reduce in real value.

Jill might want a higher return from the bank, to cover for inflation, but to get that she may be asked to deposit into a timed account, or a product that won't allow her access to the money for a year, in return for a 3% return. She invests FN100 and, at the end of the year she will get FN103, unless she wants the money back sooner.

If she needs that money back during the year, she will probably have to pay the bank a penalty because she is breaking her promise to give them the money for a year.

Let's imagine that penalty is 2%. Now, unlike Jack who only had one outcome, Jill has 2 possible outcomes. She puts in FN100 and takes out FN103 in a year's time, but if she needs the money sooner than a year, she only gets back FN98.

The investment is risky if she will need the money sooner, and not risky if she won't – if she has money in other places – so the risk is very personal (which is why we should "integrate" risk, which we talk about next). For a billionaire, it might be zero risk, as they know they will never need the money. Or if that's all the money you have, the risk could be very high. The key is that we now have two different outcomes, with a different chance of each one happening. Things may go as well as we expect, or things may go worse.

That's risk.

Everything Is Risky

This is why different types of assets or investments have different types of risk, because we may be repaid more or less than we put in. Things increase in risk if there are more ways in which the amount we get repaid can vary, and we are less able to predict which will happen.

Nothing is risk free. Everything is risky. Even nothing.

Even if I put money in that 0% savings account, it would seem risk free, but the currency might either strengthen or weaken. If it is a big currency (US dollars or Euros) that shouldn't matter too much, but if the currency you've saved in is smaller than those, like fictional Freedom Notes that don't exist, and it weakens, you will have to pay more for anything imported. Like oil. Or holidays. Or those now-even-more-expensive avocados.

Is there any way of avoiding currency risk? Well, you could invest in gold, which doesn't get affected by individual currencies, but goes up and down all the time against the US dollar – so there is still some risk there.

Nothing is risk free, because the future is not guaranteed. President Lincoln said that nothing is certain in life except death and taxes: everything else is risk.

Some investments can make more money because they will hopefully grow in the future, but there will always be additional uncertainty with that. For example, while a deposit account is guaranteed by the bank and often the government, a bond from a company will only be guaranteed by that company. If the company can't pay, you won't get that money. Also, if the bond is already trading, people will have calculated the risks of that bond, and you may buy at a time when the price is high and sell when it's low, losing you money.

The same is true of shares in companies, except there is no guarantee from the company you will even get your money back. If the company does well, you will share in its profits, but also, if everyone else expects it to do well, you will have to pay more for that share. If expectations turn against the company, even if the company does well, you may not be able to sell for as much.

The more ways there are for your investment making more money, the more ways there are for our prediction about that to be wrong – and that's what creates the risk.

Using A Lever

Another thing that creates risk, or at least is a source of risk because of the way it increases it, is "leverage," or debt. This is when we borrow to invest, such as a mortgage for buying a house. It doesn't change the predictability, but it increases the volatility – which might best be thought of as the wobbliness – of the return.

It's called leverage because it works like a lever: increasing the impact, both for the positive and the negative.

If Jill buys a house for FN100,000 and pays cash without borrowing any money at all, then if it goes up 10% in a year, she will make 10% on her investment. That's very nice. If it goes down 10%, she will lose 10%: not so nice.

If Jack doesn't have FN100,000 to buy the house he wants, he could borrow FN90,000 with a 90% mortgage, and put in a FN10,000 (10%) deposit. If, like Jill's house, the price of the house goes up 10%, Jack's FN10,000 deposit will have doubled in value to FN20,000 for a 100% return, because the price of the house will now be FN110,000 but the FN90,000 he borrowed to buy the house won't have changed. FN110,000 minus FN90,000 equals FN20,000 – that's the good side of leverage.

If the house fell 10% in value though, he would still have to pay back the 90% loan, and his down-payment of FN10,000 would have become worthless: if he sold the house for FN90,000, and paid back the FN90,000 loan, he would have nothing left. That's the bad side of leverage.

The predictability of the house going up or down 10% did not change. What changed was the size of the outcome, because Jack borrowed.

So risk is the unpredictability of the outcome, and the outcome will be unpredictable if we think about the risks or not. The key is: if we think about them and learn about them, we can manage and potentially reduce them, without reducing our return.

R for Return

Return is what we get paid by the investment in a particular period – normally a year.

- When Jack put money in the bank, with no interest, his return was zero.

- When Jill put FN100 in the bank and got FN103 after a year, the return was 3% per year.

- When Jill bought a house and it went up 10%, if she had sold it then, her return would have been 10%.

- And when it went down 10%, her return was −10%.

- When Jack bought that house with a 90% mortgage, and it went up 10%, his return was 100%.

- And when it went down 10%, his return was −100%. Ouch!

If you look at long-term market charts, it might be hard to guess what the average return has been. Sometimes they go up, sometimes they go down. Over the longer term, however, those ups and downs combine to give a more steady average.

This is true for lower risk investments but not higher risk ones. If you make investments that have the potential for you to double or lose everything, your return will not equal the average. At some point, you will lose everything, and your return will be zero. You will be wiped out and won't be able to make another investment. It's why you should avoid really high-risk investments – and casinos.

Risk = Return?

There are some formulas that show how and why, over time, you get more return for the more risk you take, but for now, just remember this: you want more return for taking more risk, because then your long-term average will at least be flat or be slightly higher.

Equally, something that is offering you higher return will probably come with more risk. If you think it doesn't, look again. And again. And again. Ask yourself, if there is so much return for such low risk, why isn't everyone investing in this?

That's what makes risk and return move closer to each other: millions of people all over the world are investing all the time, and one of the things that happens as a result is that the different risks and returns in different investments tend to move closer together. Things with low risk tend to offer low returns, and things with higher risks tend to need higher returns to make people want to take those risks.

This is a good thing, because it means, if we are careful, we should be able to understand the risks we are taking by looking at the returns we are being offered. If someone offers you a guaranteed way of making 20% per year, it's probably either a lie or illegal, because that opportunity would have already been taken by someone else. Some investments may return 20% in some years, but they will probably have lower or even negative returns in others.

The bad news is that if we want to get higher returns, to potentially double our money over time, we will have to take some more risk ... but we will learn in the next few steps how to do our best to minimise risks while maximising returns.

"Integrate" Your Investing With Your Life

So, while we now know that we can increase our returns on investment by taking more risk, we don't want that to become uncontrolled risk taking. In fact, what we most want to do is to minimise the risks we take for the returns we receive. The more we can reduce our risk with higher returns, the higher our "probable return" will be, and the faster we'll achieve our Freedom Formula.

While this is difficult, because the whole world is trying to get the most return for the smallest amount of risk, there are some ways of keeping your own risk levels as low as possible.

The next three letters in R-RISK are for just that. S for Spread is the one that financial books normally talk about, under the longer name "diversification," and is famously known as "the only free lunch in finance."

That may be true – that spreading your risks around can reduce them – but there are other ways of reducing your risk, and the one you can be most in control of yourself is I for "Integration" or "Integrity."

Because integration, like integrity, is about being true to yourself. It's investing in things where being exposed to that risk makes sense for your future, not someone else's, while also reducing risks you don't need. Although spreading your risks will help reduce them, you shouldn't spread them too far away from things that are relevant to your life.

- Take risks you need to take.

- Don't take risks you don't.

The point is that you can increase your returns and reduce your risk by making sure you take risks that you need to be exposed to, or that will benefit you, without being too exposed to risks you don't need.

The classic financial industry way of doing this is to organise your investment portfolio into global asset exposure, ensuring that roughly 70% of your investments are in the country you live in or the currency you use.

When you want to convert the investment back into the time and energy put into it, the investment will still be in the same economy that you want to buy time and energy in, so there is a greater chance that the prices of those things will have moved in a similar direction.

While the chances of us making more or less money might be the same, we haven't taken a risk that we didn't need to take by investing in a country or economy we didn't need exposure to. We shouldn't take too many risks we don't need to take. So, if we shouldn't take risks we don't need to take, we should think about the ones we do we need to take.

Where Should We Buy A House?

Let's look at one of the biggest and most important single assets you will probably want to buy in your life: a house.

You should really only buy a house if you know you want to live in that location for a very long time, perhaps the rest of your life, or if you want to return to it at a later date in your life (before which the price might have changed a lot).

If you know you will want the asset for a long time, owning it reduces the risks you might otherwise expose yourself to: if the price of houses in the area you want to live goes up a lot, then owning one has protected you from that risk; while if the price goes down, you still want the house. It's a risk you need to take.

This is why this is part of integration: we are focusing on risks we need to take, or may have no choice about taking, rather than getting distracted by thinking about returns that involve taking risks we don't need to take.

House prices are not extremely volatile day-by-day, like the stock market reports we see on the news, but they can move in just as big directions over extended periods of time. For example, lots of people think house prices in Japan are very expensive, because they remember reports from the 1980s and 1990s about how expensive they were then. But without it being in the news very much, house prices in Japan went down for more than 16 years in a row after that: a house that would have cost 200 million yen in the early 1990s would sell for less than 80 million yen 20 years later. That many of those houses would have been bought on 30-or-more-year mortgages makes the situation even worse, probably doubling the total cost, but the Japanese people can carry on living in them.

In London, the story was almost exactly the opposite. If you had bought a house in London for £100,000 (that would have been a long time ago), it would have gone up to £350,000 over the same period as the prices in Tokyo collapsed.

In many ways, as long as you want to live in the house, it really doesn't matter if it goes up in price or not; because if you're going to live in it, you won't get that money anyway.

People in Japan are living in houses that are now very cheap but used to be expensive; while people in London are living in expensive houses that used to be cheaper. They're all still living in houses, and many will keep those houses until they die. The change in the price doesn't matter so much if you want to use the asset. They could have invested in better things – that's the opportunity cost – and paid less for that asset, but it was an integral asset in their life.

This extreme example is useful because it shows the importance of integrating your investing with your life.

If you had lived in Japan in the early 1990s, and wanted to move back to London sometime later, the 200 million yen you spent on a Tokyo house would have been enough to buy you that 100,000 pound house; but if you sold it today, it would only be worth 40,000 pounds. Not only is it no longer enough to buy a 100,000-pound house, it will only just pay for a 10% deposit on the same house, because that house has gone up in price by three and a half times!

That's the point of integration. The real value of a house is it being a place to live, in the place you want to live for your whole life. If you intend to live to a very old age without wanting to work all the way to the grave, the first thing you will need to secure is a roof over your head, and that roof should be in a place you want to live for your whole life, or later in your life, not just at the moment. If you work somewhere else, then you really need to ponder if you need to buy where you are working, or if you should protect yourself from the risk that the other place you want to live later goes up in price.

You might choose to invest in other asset classes and pay rent until you die, but there is a risk that house prices and rent will increase faster than your other investments. You've taken a risk you didn't need to take there. By investing some money in property in a place you want to live your whole life or at least later in your life (when compounded prices will have made more impact), you have reduced your overall risk by integrating that risk with your life.

The more you integrate your investing with who you are, who you want to be, and how you will eventually want to spend your investments, the more you will reduce the amount of risk you are taking without necessarily reducing your returns. Buying a house somewhere you don't want to live for a long period of time is taking a risk you don't need to take.

For example, if you have a job in the city and can't afford to buy a property there, ask yourself if that's where you'll always want to live. If you think you might want to move back to your smaller (cheaper) hometown someday, then buying property there, and renting it out until you want to move back, might integrate your risks better.

"I want to live in a castle in a magical kingdom," the princess told Charlie.

"That's just as well," said Charlie, *"because sometimes not even magic can keep up with property prices!"*

Opportunity Cost

"Opportunity cost" is key to understanding risk and integration.

As we discussed at the very beginning of investing, everything we do is a choice. Even if we choose to do nothing, we are choosing NOT to do the things we could do. Whenever we compare the things we could do, what our choices are, we can see our opportunity cost: opportunity cost is the benefit of the choice we could have made.

"Imagine you have two invitations for the same evening," Charlie explained.

"Easy," said the princess. *"Let's go to both."*

"We can't," Charlie told her. *"They're at the same time and on other sides of the kingdom."*

"Ok," the princess said after pausing for thought, and clearly hoping that this was a clever answer, *"Which one will the most princes attend?"*

Charlie raised the thing above his eye that on a human would be called an eyebrow but on a frog is more of a green bump. *"One is a party for all the visiting royal princes, and the other is a talk by the most successful women entrepreneurs in the kingdom who will help you with your side-gig."*

"Wouldn't it be rude of me not go to the one with all the princes?" the princess asked, hoping, hoping ...

"Officially," Charlie sighed, *"neither answer is wrong because the exercise is to help understand opportunity cost ..."*

The princess pumped her fist in celebration.

"That doesn't make your answer right though," Charlie scolded. *"And don't ever fist-pump again. No princess should ever do that!"*

"Not even if she's an entrepreneur princess?"

Like the princess, imagine you have two invitations for the same day. Neither event can be moved, and you can only go to one. On another day, with nothing else on, you would have chosen either one, because your opportunity cost was nothing, sitting at home alone, without even a frog to chat to; but now you have to choose. That's opportunity cost: the cost of what we could have got, or done, if we hadn't chosen as we did.

We always have to choose what we do with our money, because only by making the best choices do we make our money work for us.

Let's say we have our money in a savings account that is paying 1%, and the bank offers us a new, timed deposit account where we have to lock up our money, but we will get a higher interest payment. There's one that pays 5% but locks our money up for 1 year, one that pays 3% and locks us in for 3 months, and another that pays 1.5%, and locks us up for just 1 month.

We might feel that there is too much risk in being locked up for a year, so although it pays a lot more money, that doesn't feel like an appropriate risk for us. Even the one paying 3% might be too risky, as we're not sure about needing the money in 3 months. But 1 month? We're fairly certain that we can take some of our money out of our savings and lock it up for a month and make an extra half a percent.

This is the way a portfolio should grow. Take a little more risk, and add a little more return, bit by bit. Look at the opportunity you are turning down, and measure it against what you have, and decide if you should take it or turn it down.

Maybe after a couple of months you will realise you haven't needed the money, and you can start to put some of the money into the 3-month deposit. If you stagger those inputs (i.e. a little every month), then you will have access to cash every month – just like under the 1-month deposit – but be making double the return. Your opportunity cost of 1.5% with less liquidity risk will seem small compared to the 3% you could make, and so you'll switch some money. You'll probably still have some in your savings account, just in case, but now you'll be making 3 times the return. Rather than your money doubling in 72 years, now you'll be doubling in 25.

And eventually you'll move on to the 5% deposit, and then on to other asset classes, all the time looking at the risk-return scenario, comparing it to the opportunity you could get, and deciding where you can add a little extra risk to get a little extra return.

"Opportunity cost" is the tool you use to decide how to make these decisions. Make sure you are always finding out about new investment opportunities – savings accounts, stocks and shares, bonds, insurance policies – and then decide which risk-return scenario is best for you by comparing all of the opportunities.

More integration, less risk

So, if we know we are going to live in a particular country, we can invest in that economy and we can buy property in that market. Are there other ways of integrating our investments with our expected lives to reduce risk? I think there are lots.

The simplest way to work that out is to determine how we expect to spend our money. Housing is probably the biggest expenditure for all of us, and so buying a house will integrate that risk with your lifestyle. That could be followed by other consumption, like food, travel, transport or insurance costs.

Can we integrate our investments with these other costs of living?

We can do it quite simply by making equity investments in the shares of the companies that operate in these sectors. If we're worried that travel or transport costs might increase, which is normally due to an increase in oil prices, we could invest in oil companies, which generally increase in value when there's an oil price spike. An index fund or exchange traded fund (ETF) might remove the difficulty of choosing the best one for you and keep the costs down. It would also protect us against the impact of a big spike in oil prices pushing through into the rest of our cost of living in things like food and general shopping.

What happens if oil prices go down? Well, those investments won't do so well, but our cost of living will likely not increase so much either, as our transport costs won't increase. And over time we can potentially increase our investments in oil companies when oil prices are low, and decrease them when oil prices go up ...

If we expect to spend a lot of money shopping (we have had this conversation already!), then we could invest in consumer companies or retailers that will make a profit from our shopping. We need to be careful doing this, as retail formats that are popular today may be less popular in the future, but you might be able to find an index that collects the popular ones together, and that could mean that you have a portfolio of investments that goes up in line with your spending potential – or even ahead of it.

You could buy shares in the companies that make the things your favourite shops sell, no matter what it is, fashion brands, soap, biscuits or computers. Or you could make an investment in ecommerce companies if you think that the future will all be online and that's where you're going to spend your money.

If you bought a house with a mortgage, and the mortgage payments are quite a large part of your spending, you can even buy shares in that bank, or a collection of other banks. If the interest rate goes up (banks generally make more profits with higher interest rates), it is very likely that the bank's share price will increase and so you will have an investment that could help cover your higher cost of living.

And if you can't afford to buy the house you want to live in, or indeed any house, then there are investments called **Real Estate Investment Trusts** that invest in property for you, and manage it for you, and pay you a pretty high share of the rent, and tend to go up in value if the value of property goes up.

Do you see? Adding new investments doesn't have to be about purely adding new risks. You can take some risks which have returns that match off other unavoidable risks you have taken without knowing it: the risk that you will have to eat more expensive food in the future, drive a car with more expensive oil, or live in an area where housing has become more expensive, or that your mortgage costs will increase.

Focus on what you think your life might look like, and see if you can take some risks that will match that, and you will be successfully integrating your investing with your life and reducing your risk as a result.

If we think back to "Wizard Warren's" advice at the beginning of this chapter, that's essentially what he was doing. He advised investing 90% of our assets into an index fund, and that index fund will include banks, oil companies, food companies, airlines, technology and all the things you are likely to use.

Taken a step further, if you have a particular belief, such as protecting the environment, you can integrate your portfolio with that by only investing in companies or sectors you believe do good for the world, such as healthcare, education and clean energy.

S Is For Spread

"Don't put all your eggs in one basket" is probably the oldest saying in the book, and it has survived because it's true. Financial theory argues about most things but one of the very few it agrees on is that "diversification is the only free lunch in investing". What that means is that if you put your eggs in one basket, you're paying for lunch. S is for Spreading your risks around between different baskets, because it will result in less risky returns.

The key to understanding "diversification" is that you don't need to avoid risk to reduce risk. In fact, making two risky investments can be less risky than making one investment, even if that one investment seems less risky. How?

For example, if we invest in a property and it is successful, it would seem to be efficient to invest in another similar property nearby; but if that street was attacked by a dragon, both our properties would be scorched. A property in a different street or town would reduce the risk of that happening. A property in a different country would be exposed to the risks in that country, which could come from its economy, its currency or its politics, but they probably wouldn't be risks you need to take.

Investing in things other than property would expose you to non-property risks. Maybe the government in your country will raise interest rates, and property prices will drop as people can't pay their mortgages. Maybe all countries will do that, and property prices will fall all over the world, so non-property assets will do better. Maybe owning shares in banking companies would do better.

Having all your eggs in one basket can be risky, but the answer isn't a safer basket. It's a second basket, and a third and maybe a fourth. What should those baskets be? Let's build them up steadily.

The First Safe Basket

We started out putting our money in a savings account, didn't we? That's our emergency fund. That may not need to be diversified, but we can, if we want, diversify that by keeping some of our emergency funds in a second account in a different bank, or a different form of saving account that maybe has some restrictions but pays a higher rate. You might also choose to keep some cash somewhere safe in the house. Not a lot, but just in case.

These are the first times we've spread our risk around, and we can see immediately that we haven't reduced our "risk" directly. In many ways we've increased the number of different risks we're exposed to, because we have cash in the house that might be stolen, and savings in two banks, either of which could get into trouble, or not. It seems as though we've taken extra risks; but we haven't, because we have reduced our exposure to those individual risks. If something terrible happened to one of those savings, we would still be ok, hopefully, with the other ones.

A Gold And Silver Basket

But what if the currency our emergency fund is in, our home currency, weakens?

"How would that happen?" asked the princess.

"Remember that money can be just pieces of paper with a picture of the emperor on them? If he prints more, then the value of each little piece of paper could go down."

The princess shuddered at the thought of even more pictures of the naked emperor. "Yes," she said, "who would want those?"

Well, we might be ok to start with, as prices will still be the same as before for a while, but soon prices will start to go up as imports cost more money in our now weaker currency.

We might think about saving in a foreign currency (people who live in countries with volatile currencies often save in US dollars), it's also worth considering gold and silver as alternative options. Because gold and silver are generally valued in US dollars, if it's just our currency that has weakened, the value of the gold we bought should now be worth more in that currency. So we've made money taking that extra risk. And as I said before, feel a bit like a pirate.

More Risk More Return Baskets

Now we have two safer baskets, we will also want some baskets that grow faster. We might want to buy some property, but as it can take some time to save up for the deposit on a property, we should probably start with an equity investment basket.

As we discussed in "Integration," we can invest in assets that integrate with our lives. If we live in a big city and can't afford to buy property there yet, but really want to, investing in a Real Estate Investment Trust (REIT) in that city would be a way of slowly building up an investment that could turn into a deposit on a house, but also has similar risks to that deposit – so you will have aligned your risks, thus reducing them. Perhaps you would also like some banks or consumer or tech companies, or an index like the S&P500 which tracks the 500 largest companies in the US, or an exchange traded fund (ETF), which tracks that index. That's your equity basket.

As you add more investments to your portfolio, and the investments are of a different type, even though you might think that the investments themselves are becoming riskier, the combination of all the different risks will make your portfolio safer.

One way to think of building an investment portfolio is to think of it like a wardrobe. Although you may like white T-shirts more than any other item, a coat will be better in winter and a jacket will be good for formal occasions. The more spread you get into your wardrobe, the better prepared you will be for any occasion.

It's the same with your portfolio. While it makes sense to build your portfolio around things you know, and around your life, it is important to spread your investments sensibly, to take on different types of risks.

Then, when a dragon scorches the street, you won't lose all of your assets.

Magic Trick 2: A Little At A Time

Another way to integrate your investing with your lifestyle is to invest a little at a time.

Some people don't invest because they think they need to have a lot of money to invest. Maybe they think that investing a little here and there isn't the way they should invest, that professionals do it differently. But they're wrong. Professionals do exactly that by "dollar cost averaging," and it's one of the best tricks in investing.

Imagine you have FN600 to invest in something over a six-month period, but rather than investing it all in one day, you buy FN100 every month. If your target investment is an index fund priced at FN10, for example, you might buy 10 units in January. If the price went down to FN5 in February, you would buy 20 units. If the price went up to FN20 in March, you would buy 5 units, and so on.

After 3 months, you have 35 units. If you had bought 35 units in January, it would have cost you FN350, but you've only spent FN300, because when the units were cheaper (February), you bought more and when they were more expensive (March) you bought less. You didn't buy more or less deliberately – it's just because you spent the same amount of money every month that you got different amounts of the investment.

Dollar cost averaging shows that it makes sense to invest regularly in small numbers, not large amounts, so don't feel you need a big lump sum to make it worthwhile.

By starting early and making small investments you can use both the magic tricks of compounding and dollar cost averaging to make your fortune.

K is for Knowledge

So, when we started learning about investing, we knew we wanted to make more money with our savings. That's called Return on Investment. We also learned that higher returns generally come with higher risks, and we learned about R-RISK.

R-R for Risk-Return, and then "Integrating" our investments with our lives and "Spreading" our investments across different asset classes, different companies, different countries. All of these things help us get better returns while managing our risk.

And what we've been doing through this process is the last part of R-RISK – we've been adding to our "Knowledge," which is the most important part of investing.

The more you know, the more you can do. And the more you do, the more you can learn, because one of the best ways of learning about investing is to learn by doing. You should learn about investing by investing. You will care more about your learning if you have what writer and investor Nicholas Nassim Taleb calls "skin in the game." We learn best when we have something to win or something to lose.

Decide which way you want to integrate your investing with your life next, or in what way you want to diversify your investing. Decide on a new type of asset, and then learn as much about it as you can before you start to make that investment.

If you can't do this homework about a particular asset, you probably shouldn't be risking your future lifestyle by investing in it. If you want that future, you should be prepared to learn about it. You can start with either the practicalities or the theory. You need to learn both.

1. Learn The Theory ...

The theory is how to value an investment, whether it's a good time to invest in the sector, and whether a specific investment of that type is good.

For example, if you're looking at investing in property, you will want to learn about rental yield in the different real estate categories (commercial or residential) and about historic price performance. You can check if different areas and different types of property have made better returns in the past and assess what kind of returns they will make in the future. That's the theory.

Every asset class has a different set of theories to learn. Some basic skills transfer across asset classes, such as understanding the "cash flow," but there will be different words, different techniques, different risks. Enjoy this. Don't be worried by things you don't know when you start. If you take advantage of online resources, you can learn more through your own investing than you ever can from an expensive degree.

One amazing resource that is currently free is the Chartered Financial Institute's Investment Foundations course, run by the most respected organisation in investing. If you pass the exam, you even get a free certificate: https://www.cfainstitute.org/en/programs/investment-foundations.

2. And The Practicalities

The practicalities of an investment are the specifics of how you can, or should, make the investment. For real estate, you need to ask about rents, mortgages and tenant law. Ask about selling prices. Ask about commission rates, property tax rates, stamp duty rates. Ask more than one person. Ask lots.

In all forms of investment, there are costs of making the investment. This can include things like the commission you pay to the person who brought you the deal (this could be a real estate or insurance agent, or stock broker or even a bank), and importantly it can include things such as government charges like stamp duty or tax. The tax may be there up-front, when you make the purchase, it could come in later, every year on your property, or on its rent, or at the end when you come to sell, via capital gains tax. All of these factors will affect your return and need to be understood.

Knowledge is crucial, and learning is never-ending. Our investing wizard, Warren Buffet, has a famous quote that says: "If you've been playing poker for half an hour and you still don't know who the patsy is, you're the patsy." "Patsy" is Warren Buffet's word for fool, or sucker, but the key here is that the patsy is the person who is going to lose money because they don't have enough knowledge. Make sure it isn't you by doing your research.

Do you need to go so far in your knowledge as to be able to calculate the spreads on bond curves, or project free cash flows in your target investment? No, you don't have to, but the closer you get to those levels, the more you will be able to sit at a poker table and work out that someone else is the patsy, and that

WHICH STEP IS RIGHT FOR YOU?

There are seven steps to investing like a seven dollar millionaire, and we can climb them like a ladder. Look at the ladder from the bottom to the top, read the descriptions on each step and decide which step you're on. Tick the box on the right.

Then take another look at the ladder, perhaps reading each step from the top to the bottom. This time decide which step you'd like to be on, and tick the relevant box on the right. Now you know what your investment journey should look like.

STEP 7
I really enjoy learning about investing, and have a high risk appetite. *(active investor in growth asset class, like equities and property)*

STEP 6
I'm young and understand I can take risks, but I'm not ready yet to do it all on my own. *(combined passive and active investor in mainly growth assets)*

STEP 5
I've investment funds and I'm prepared to take on some more risk, but I really want to minimise losses. *(passive investor across diversified assets)*

STEP 4
I have investment funds, but I don't like risk. *(passive investor in mainly defensive assets)*

STEP 3
I have no debt and an emergency fund, I'm ready to start getting higher returns from indexes. *(passive investor)*

STEP 2
I have some savings and I'm building my emergency fund and paying off any debt. *(pre-investor - cash)*

STEP 1
I don't have any savings, let alone investments. *(pre-investor)*

Mark where you are now with a tick, and then mark where you want to climb to.

Figure 6.2

you should go ahead and invest. You'll learn about new areas for investing you didn't know about before, and you'll learn to assess the difference between scams and really great opportunities.

Perhaps the most important practicality is to understand who you are, and what stage of your investing journey you are on. In *The Thousand Dollar Journal* we looked at this journey as a ladder, going up levels as you learn more and become more comfortable with different investments and their associated risks.

Step 1: "I don't have any savings to invest. I don't even have an emergency fund yet. What should I do now?"

Don't think too much about investing, as you don't have any money to invest. Start saving. Saving and investing isn't like debating if the chicken or the egg came first.

Saving always comes first – before spending and before investing too.

The most important thing for you on this step is to learn saving habits to build an emergency fund. Your emergency fund will rescue you from danger, and that could be more valuable than an investment fund. Learning this will take all your energy, and until you're a successful saver, there's no point in trying to become a successful investor.

You're a pre-investor. Start saving now so you have something to invest in later steps.

Step 2: "I'm saving an emergency fund, but I have debts and have never invested before. What should I do now?"

First, you can continue building your emergency fund, putting more of it in a savings account or time deposit that pays more interest. That way you can earn slightly higher returns on the money you don't need immediately. That's the most basic lesson of investing:

money you don't need immediately can be used to make higher returns.

Second, you need to start paying off your debts. Debt nearly always has a higher rate of interest than a deposit, so paying off debts will save you more money than you could otherwise make. Also, the debt has been guaranteed, by YOU, so it's a certain payment, rather than an uncertain return on investments. This means you should pay it off as fast as you can.

You're still a pre-investor, but your first investment asset is cash.

Step 3: "I have no debt, an emergency fund and a small amount of money in a savings account. What should I do now?"

You're ready to start your investing career. You need to do two things: decide where to invest and what in.

1. Find an online broker. Google *best online broker* and your country. Go to all of their websites and ask them lots of questions in their online chatrooms. Ask them about the cost of investing. Don't invest in anything that costs more than 1% ($10 of your $1,000 investment).

Google Charles Schwab, Fidelity, Vanguard and robo-advisor.

In Singapore and Hong Kong, you can look up Fundsupermart or Stashaway, or take a look at the Start Investing Now page on our website (https://www.sevendollarmillionaire.com/start-here/) for updated links direct to reliable platforms.

Decide what to invest in. If you're American, you should buy a fund that tracks the S&P500. It's the most important index in the world, following 500 of the biggest companies. If you invest in it, you get the world's top 500 CEOs working for you!

If you're not American, you should also buy the S&P500 adding an index from your own area for some of your investing money. If you're Filipino, you could add a fund following the PSEi – or a bigger index, like MSCI Asia. If you're British, the FTSE100 will do a similar job.

You're now a passive investor. Well done!

Step 4. "I don't want to think too much about my investments. It scares me. What should I do?"

First, keep adding to your investments slowly, perhaps on a regular monthly savings scheme, so that you gain from "cost averaging." Build slowly and learn more as you invest.

Second, invest more widely to diversify your risks, so you don't need to worry so much. You can add different equities indexes, like the Nasdaq if you like technology or European or Asian indexes if you want fewer American stocks. You can even invest in the MSCI World Index which will cover everything. And non-equities indexes like bonds should go up if your equities indexes go down.

You don't need to do this all in one go. Maybe add a new index every three or six months. You're now a steady, passive investor, with diversified assets. Look at you!

Step 5. "I've saved a lot of money that I don't want to lose, but I am still nervous about investing. What should I do?"

As your investment portfolio grows, you may get nervous about the risk of your nest egg dropping in value.

This doesn't mean you should switch everything into defensive assets like cash and bonds though. You may need your money for much longer than you think, and if your returns don't beat inflation, their real value will go down over time: although you might have the same number, it might not buy so much in the shops.

If you're nervous, and already wealthy, keep one year of spending as cash or in a savings account. Then you can afford to keep the rest in widely diversified growth assets, which will pay you a "yield" to boost your cash levels.

Step 6. "I'm young and understand that I can take more risks. What should I do?"

You can take more risk as you should be able to survive through a cycle, or perhaps even two, without touching your investments. Other than your emergency fund, all your money should be in growth assets like equity indexes.

Once you have enough funds to start buying property, even just a small deposit on a very small place, google *house hacking* to see if you can start building your property empire today, or even live for free!

Investing in property is a specialised skill, however, and you'll need to learn a lot of new skills before you invest. You need to learn about property markets, rental income and costs, tax and borrowing mortgages.

Do your homework for a long time before you put your money in. But when you do, you'll be an active investor in growth assets.

Step 7. "I've really enjoyed learning about investing and have a high risk appetite. What should I do now?"

You're ready to be a fully active investor in growth assets. This could mean many different things, but the two most common ways would be to start learning how to select and invest in individual companies that you expect to outperform the index, and "house hacking" to build up a property portfolio.

The key to both is that they're "active" investments – that is, you're doing them yourself and not passively following someone else's fund or index.

Active investors sometimes do much better than passive investors. They can sometimes time a property market perfectly, and double their money, or buy a "fixer-upper" that sells for more when renovated. They can also sometimes invest in companies that do much better than the index, and more than double their money.

The Simplest Investment Portfolio

If you still want to have a general idea of the kind of investment portfolio you should be aiming for, we think this is the simplest, most generally applicable portfolio.

- Aim to have about 6 months of your spending in a liquid investment emergency fund, with a mix of current accounts, savings accounts, time deposits and gold. You don't have to get it up to 6 months immediately, you can start at 3.

- Focus next on index funds or ETFs that reduce your cost of access to capital markets. These should preferably be the S&P500 to start and then perhaps other markets, if you need exposure to them. If you get to 90% of your assets in these assets, you have replicated Wizard Warren's 90/10 portfolio recommendation. That's a great place to be.

- After that, you can slowly add individual stocks or sectors when you feel comfortable, in small numbers at first.

- If you really want to own property, but it is too expensive where you live, you could add some local REITs to those funds.

- If you live in a high-yield property market, more than 4%, aim to own at least one house, if not two: see if the numbers work for "house-hacking" where you live.

- Make sure all of these investments are as tax efficient as possible, by taking advantage of your country's tax-free investing and savings structures.

Back In The Real World: Avoiding Scams

As you learn to invest, you'll hear about new things. That's good, because some of this new information will be genuinely good things. Unfortunately, some will be rip-offs. It's worth noting here that scams are MUCH more dangerous than risky investments, because you will lose all of your capital in a scam. Compared to a bad stock market, which may fall 10% or 20% in a year, a scammer will take all of the money you give them – and come back for more.

Here are some quick ways to spot the scams.

- If it looks too good to be true, you should assume it is a lie. High returns, as we discussed, usually come with higher risks. That's fine when you want to take those risks, but someone who promises high returns without high risks is probably hiding something. They may be hiding a risk that they don't want you to know about, or maybe just the risk that they may steal your money. Just as bad, they may not know the risks themselves. Avoid them.

- Similarly, the word "guarantee," although it is often used to overcome investors' nervousness, should make you scared. Scammers use the word to make novice investors feel more comfortable, but proper investments don't carry a guarantee, they carry risk – that's how they can offer returns. Avoid offers of high guaranteed returns.

- Ask lots of questions. Ask anything you want to ask. Ask for their license to sell to you, or for their industry accreditation. Importantly, ask why they're telling you about such a good deal. Did you call them or did they call you? If they called you, ask them why. If you were a broker, you would give your best deals to your biggest clients, where you will make the most money and win their loyalty. So why is someone you don't know offering you something so good?

- A specific type of scam called "Ponzi" or "pyramid" schemes rely on new people putting in new money to pay earlier subscribers (they aren't investors). If you can't work out how your investment is making a return, there is a chance you are buying into a pyramid, which will eventually collapse. Real investments make returns. Houses make money from the value of property going up and from rental income: the same thing for shares in companies. If you can't see where the investments are being made and the returns are coming from, assume it's a pyramid and avoid it.

- MOST IMPORTANT: Don't feel rushed, or guilty or embarrassed. This is your money they want, so you should feel patient, calm and confident. You are the boss. If they give you a gift, it's probably a trick to make you feel guilty; either refuse to take the gift if it will make you feel guilty, or take it and forget about it. You don't have to do anything with your money you don't want to.

Where to Begin Investing

Knowing what assets to invest in can seem bewildering to start with, but once you decide what you're going to buy, you realise you also need to decide where – what platform or service provider you are going to use.

The simplest option will often be to use the investment platform offered by your bank, as your money is already there and you apparently trust them enough to keep your money there, so that's the trust part covered too.

Banks are also getting better at keeping up with the more innovative products that "fintech" (financial technology) companies offer via their apps or websites, such as roboadvisers that can simplify your investment process or enhance your choices and experience.

But fintech apps and other service providers are generally more at the cutting edge of making these things simpler – so there is a constantly changing selection of different investment platforms to choose from, and that changing selection is different in every country in the world as different financial jurisdictions have different rules and different entry requirements.

This complexity is why we created the Start Here page on our website – www.sevendollarmillionaire. com/start-here – to be an introductory guide to what apps and services we have tried, or people we know have tried. It should be a good place for you to start.

I Think I Can See The End Of The Woods!

We have moved from 0% savings to 45% savings in the previous four chapters, and assuming that we can earn an investment return of 7%, then we have moved from never being free to having to work for only 21 years before having the rest of our lives free. This is how quickly we might get out of the woods.

In all the previous stages we have considered how much improvement we could get from the lessons learned in the chapter before. This time, we are going to consider the importance of investing well.

All of the formulas we use in this book for investing assume a return of 7%, because this is achievable by investing in a range of assets: it assumes an inflation rate of 3%, and investments that outperform that by 4%.

If our investments didn't earn 4% above inflation, and instead only kept pace with inflation, 3% returns, our forest would go back to looking like this, even if we did save 40% of our income:

Instead of being free after just 21 years, if we don't invest well, we will be free after only 31 years. That's free at 51 instead of 41. Gaining an additional 4% of return, not a huge amount, has given us 10 extra years of freedom.

This is how important it is to invest early and well.

Investing early will mean we take advantage of the magic of compounding.

Investing well will mean that our assets compound at a rate faster than inflation, and we will be out of the woods much faster.

Are You Ready For *Happy Ever After?*

Did you invest enough in this chapter to be able to answer these questions?

1. **If you put FN10,000 in an investment with a 7% return, it will be worth FN20,000 in _____ years' time.**

    a) 5.

    b) 8.5.

    c) 10.

    d) Never, because I will take it out next week and spend it.

2. **If you leave that investment there for a total of 30 years, how much will the FN10,000 become?**

    a) FN30,000.

    b) FN80,000.

    c) One MILLION dollars.

3. **What do the two Rs stand for in R-RISK:**

    a) Rest and Relaxation.

    b) Risk and Return.

    c) Retire and Regret.

4. **Which of these are good ways to integrate your investments with the way you live?**

    a) Buy a house somewhere you want to live for a long time.

    b) Invest in the currency you mainly spend.

    c) Invest in industries and commodities that take up a lot of your spending.

    d) All of the above.

5. **Are 5 risky investments safer or riskier than just one risky investment?**

   a) Riskier.

   b) Safer.

   c) Safer, as long as the risks are all different.

6. **What's your opportunity cost?**

   a) 5 dollars.

   b) 6%.

   c) The next best thing you could be doing.

7. **What's the best way to avoid being scammed when investing?**

   a) Ask lots of questions.

   b) Understand where your money is going, and how you get a return on it.

   c) Don't believe anything that seems too good to be true, or says it is guaranteed.

   d) Doing all of the above, and more!

Answers

1. c) 10: 7% doubles in 10 years.
2. b) FN10,000 becomes FN80,000 in 30 years at just a 7% return.
3. b) Risk and return.
4. d) All of the above.
5. c)
6. c)
7. d)

A Tax Break

It can often feel like the rich get all the breaks – particularly the tax breaks. Although we can't afford to employ the armies of accountants and lawyers that rich people use to get their breaks, we can spend a bit of time on Google to make sure we make our life is as tax efficient as it can be.

I want to make one thing clear: it is our duty and legal responsibility to pay tax in almost every country in the world. Just like the rich, though, it's not our duty to pay the maximum amount of tax payable. It is our duty to pay the minimum.

While the difference in tax might not pay for expensive advisors, it could still change our investing. Let's say the maximum rate where you live is 40%, and the minimum you might have to pay is 25%. The difference is equal to 15% of your income. If you can switch that into saving, going from 10% saving to 25% saving, it could be the difference between being free at 72, and being free at 53 – almost 19 years of work for a bit of tax efficiency.

That's the importance of tax, or at least it could be, if you learn to think about it properly.

1. **The Income Tax Break:** unless you live in Monaco or Brunei, it's very likely that you will have to pay some tax on your income. How do

you make sure you don't pay more than necessary? Take advantages of all reliefs, expense anything you can, and if necessary, use the most efficient structure, which might mean setting up a company, for example, if you are self-employed.

2. **The Saving Tax Break:** lots of governments want to encourage savings, so they offer special accounts for savers to use which will enable them to take the savings out tax free later. In the UK these are called "ISAs" or individual savings accounts, and in the US IRAs or individual retirement accounts. To encourage them even more, governments and employers sometimes match the payments made into these accounts. Yes, free money. Get some.

3. **The Investing Tax Break:** remember that we want to make an investment return of at least 7%, which is achievable. If we have to pay tax of 30% on the income of our investments, then we will need to earn a return of 10%, which is quite a lot harder and riskier. There are, however, many different ways of achieving a lower tax rate on your investing. This will become part of your "integration" process over time, working out what is the right strategy for you.

"Now that is one cool cat."

How To Own One Cool Cat

Charlie the frog joined the princess looking out of her castle window, to see what they could learn from the people below.

"Now that is one cool cat," he said.

"Who? Where?" asked the princess.

"You see the boy walking out of town, with all of his belongings in a bag over his shoulder?"

"Yes. I see him. Is he really cool? Should I marry him and live happy ever after?"

"What is wrong with you?" Charlie croaked. "First, no, marrying someone is not the way to become happy ever after and second, look at him .... He's clearly under-age!"

"Oh. Sorry," the princess mumbled.

"And anyway, I really was talking about the cat."

The princess looked again, and saw that a black and white cat was walking beside the boy – or was the boy walking beside the cat? It was hard to tell, the cat was so confident. "That is a pretty cool cat," she had to agree, "but where are they going, and why are they leaving the magic kingdom?"

"Well," said Charlie, "That's Dick Whittington, and if I'm not wrong, he's leaving to find fame and fortune in London, where he will eventually become Lord Mayor not just once or twice, but three times."

The princess stared quizzically at the talking frog. "And how do you know all that?"

"What? You can accept that a frog can talk, but my ability to see into the future is a step too far?"

"Ok, but why does Dick Whittington become so rich and famous?"

"Well, the impressive thing about Dick," Charlie tells her, *"is that he has learned a lot of the lessons we have been discussing. Although he has heard that the streets of London are paved with gold, he doesn't believe that and he knows he doesn't really have any skills that anyone will pay a lot of money for. His best chance is to get a poorly paid job working as a servant in a rich man's house, which is exactly what he will do for the first few years."*

"That doesn't sound like such a great plan to me," said the princess.

"We all have to start somewhere," said Charlie. *"I started out as a talking tadpole, and Dick will have to start at the bottom too. The good thing is, he knows it, and has a plan to get ahead, which is where the cat comes in."*

"Really?"

"Absolutely. Being a servant is just going to be Dick's day job. In his evenings off and weekends, he will have a side-gig offering the cat's services clearing houses of rats and mice. That cat is an excellent mouser, and while the streets of London aren't paved with gold, they are definitely plagued by rats. While Dick's regular job is enough to keep him alive, he saves and invests so much from his rat-catching business that he can buy up more businesses, owns houses all over the kingdom, has enough assets that he no longer needs to work and eventually they make him Lord Mayor of London three times."

"Really?" the princess repeated.

"Yes, really, you can make enough money to never need to work again. You need to save it and invest it until you have twenty-five times your spending ..."

"No. I meant, really, you talked when you were a tadpole?"

The Chapter 7 Cheat Sheet

How We Own This!

1. Freedom means owning your own life, owning your own decisions, which means you need to own this process. Only you can make this happen for you – no one else is going to help.

2. Debt means you don't own your assets, the lender does, and so you aren't yet free. Make careful decisions about when to borrow, for what, and from whom. You should only borrow for things that will definitely pay back.

3. The Freedom Formula is the equation that tells you how you can really own your own life. Twenty-five times your annual spending and you are free.

4. Income is good, but saving is better, as it has twice the impact:

   a. What you save adds to your total assets.

   b. What you save you don't spend, which cuts your annual spending calculation, which reduces the amount you need to save.

5. It doesn't always need to be 25X, but most of the time, that's the right number.

6. *Happy Ever After* means forever. The Freedom Formula doesn't mean you just hope to have more than you will need to spend ... it should keep growing as you get older to cover for inflation.

7. So: when do we start?

CHAPTER 7
Three Os For Ownership

Own The Process

A big part of being free is that this is your future. Your own. You own it. That means you have to own the process of creating your own financial freedom. Only you can do this. You cannot trust anyone else to do this for you, whether they know more about finance than you or not.

The reason you can't trust anyone to do this for you is because it isn't as important to anyone else as it is to you, or it shouldn't be. This is your future, not theirs. It's your freedom, not theirs. At some point in the future, it is highly likely your life will depend on this. The number of years you need to work will depend on it. Your happiness may well depend on this.

In the best case, the quality of your whole life will depend on this: you may manage to make enough money investing that you can cruise the world on a constant holiday, staying in luxury hotels and seeing the most amazing sights this beautiful planet has to offer. That may be your idea of *Happy Ever After*.

Or you may be able to grow old happy in the knowledge your children will have enough money to avoid poverty for their whole lives. Or you may just be able to stop worrying, knowing you are going to be ok financially.

Whatever you think a good life should be, whatever *Happy Ever After* means to you, you should be able to create it by saving and investing well.

In the worst case, it may be that your life will depend on it at the most basic level. If you fall sick and cannot work, you will know where your food is coming from, where you will live. If you haven't owned this process, you may not have enough money to live. You may need to rely on a government or charity to help you. Imagine if they won't ...

This is your life. You need to own the process of making it successful, and while money is not the only way of judging a successful life (personally, I don't think it's a good way), having enough money can enable you to make the best choices that let you live your version of a successful life.

You might want to work in charity.

Maybe you would like to teach.

Maybe you want to paint paintings or sing songs or coach sports.

Whatever you want to do, until you have financial freedom, your choices will be dictated by money.

And that's why you must OWN the process of earning, saving and investing to make yourself free. If you have read all the parts up to here, you now know what the basic tools are. You need to put them into action.

Learn To Own

More than anything, you need to be prepared to keep learning. As we discussed in R-RISK, that K for Knowledge is a key means of reducing your risk – and you need to do research at every stage. This is much easier than ever before because of the Internet: you don't have to hope your library has the latest investment books, and you don't have to knock on the door of every bank branch to find out what their services are. Everything is readily available. Read up, seek out advice, learn more.

One great thing about investing is that you don't have to become an expert on everything at the same time. If you're at the stage of going from a savings account to time deposits, find out everything you can about them online. See who is going to pay you the most, without taking risks you don't want to take. You don't need to know about commodity derivatives to do this. You only need to know about time deposits.

If you want to buy gold, find out who has the lowest spread (that's the difference between the price you pay and the price they will buy back at – the main cost in trading gold). When you invest in equities, learn about one market at a time, one fund at a time, one company at a time. When you want to invest in property, learn about and calculate the yields on different types of properties in different areas you might be interested in.

What Do You Really Own?

Ownership can mean very different things to different people, so in this second part of Owning we are going to be really clear about when you truly own something, and when you don't ... which is when you have borrowed to buy it.

That's the bad news: if you borrow to buy something, that thing still belongs to whoever lent you the money, not you. If we are going to borrow to buy things, which we probably are at some point, we have to learn to recognise what is worth borrowing to own, at what price, and what really isn't.

The better news is that sometimes the best form of investment can be paying off the debt on something you feel you already own, rather than a separate form of investment (which will have risks the debt doesn't have), so we will look at some key methods for paying down debt.

And then, lastly, let's talk about how, if we've already got a lot of debt, we are worse off than people who don't – but how that doesn't make the M.I.S.S.I.O.N. impossible. It will take more time, but it shouldn't take any more discipline than it does for people without debt.

Financial Net Worth

The money you borrowed to buy things doesn't belong to you. Whether you borrowed to buy a house, a university degree or fancy consumer goods, that money has to be paid back, and so you have to subtract the value of your debt from your total assets to know your "financial net worth."

What you really own is the total current value of all the assets you have bought, minus all the debt you still have left to repay.

In accountancy it is called the balance sheet equation: equity (what we really own) equals assets (all our stuff) minus liabilities (what we owe). You don't really own stuff if you've borrowed to buy it: the bank, or whoever you borrowed the money from, owns it.

Most people encounter the word "equity" either when looking at buying a house or when investing in the stock market (another word for stocks and shares is "equities") and it's probably most easily explained when looking at a house.

When you buy a house with a mortgage, you normally have to make a deposit of a certain percentage of the total value. For example, if you borrow 90% of the value of the house, your deposit will be 10%, so when you start, your equity will be 10%, because equity equals assets minus liabilities (debt). Your equity, or what you really own, is the total value minus what you have to pay back.

The reason it is important to point out the difference between equity and debt is because they are very different in nature. Debt needs to be paid back as a fixed amount.

If you borrow FN90,000, you have to pay back FN90,000, plus interest. If you have borrowed that money to buy a house, and its price goes down in value, from FN100,000 to FN90,000, what you really own is worth zero: your equity has no value.

That's why "what you own" doesn't include things you have borrowed to buy.

Is There Good Debt?

If you borrow 90% of the value of a house and it goes up in value by 10%, you double your money: good outcome. And if the value of the house goes down 10%, you lose all your money: bad outcome. If we want to understand when there are good times to borrow, we need to understand how we get the first good outcome and not that second bad one.

First, as we learnt in investing, although there are no guarantees, there are two key ways of improving your chances, lowering your risk, and so we need to establish what those are.

1. Make sure you are getting the lowest cost debt you can.

2. Only buy things that will make you money, preferably much more than the cost of your debt.

The first is the simplest.

1. Don't borrow money from anyone unless it's really, really cheap debt. The best example here is mortgage debt, which, wherever you are in the world, banks will normally lend to you at a very low interest rate. That's because they expect the value of the property to increase over time, and so even if you can't pay the debt, they can sell the house (note that I'm not saying *your* house – because it is still the bank's house if you have a mortgage) and recover their loan.

All other forms of lending are normally more expensive than mortgages and should be avoided. Perhaps the only people who will lend money to you at the same or lower rate than a bank issuing a mortgage are your parents or other family members.

How cheap is cheap? It should be around the level of inflation, or a tiny bit more. Remember "The Law Of 72"? It tells you how quickly a rate of return (or rate of interest) will double by dividing 72 by that number ... so a 7.2% interest rate will double in 10 years.

That is how debt ruins lives.

Borrow FN100,000 at 7.2% for 10 years, and you will have to repay FN200,000. Borrow for 20 years and you will have to repay FN400,000. Borrow for 30 years, and you will have to repay FN800,000.

To keep the numbers simple, a mortgage loan at an interest rate of 3.6% (half of 7.2%), will double every 20 years instead of every 10, so if you borrow FN100,000 for 20 years, you will owe FN200,000. Compared to borrowing at 7.2%, that's FN200,000 cheaper on a FN100,000 loan, for just a few percentage points difference. That's why you get the cheapest loan you can.

Lots of loans, including mortgages, start with lower rates, called "teaser rates," and then convert to more expensive rates later. Before you sign up for one of these, make sure you will be able to refinance by switching to another lender later, if that would be cheaper, and when they will allow that. That's one way to make sure you don't pay too much over the life of the loan.

If you don't, that kind of difference can ruin your life.

2. The next one is a bit harder: make sure you only buy things with loans that make you money.

Loans are not gifts – they have to be paid back – and as we saw above, we have to pay back more than we borrowed, perhaps double or even four times what we borrowed. This is really only possible if the thing we buy with the loan makes money or goes up in price somehow or other. If you buy something that doesn't make you more money than the cost of borrowing, or goes up in value more than the loan, borrowing is a really, really bad idea.

Let's look at five examples: a house, a car, a business, stuff or a college degree.

The House Of Your Dreams?

Buying a house is the obvious one. Over the long term, houses tend to increase in price by at least the rate of inflation, which is the base of any lending rate. Second, houses can either be lived in (reducing your cost of living) or rented out (bringing in income) and so you can save or make money to pay off your debt. It's why this is such a common form of borrowing – because it often makes sense.

The Car Of Your Nightmares?

Buying a car is another common use of debt, but it makes a lot less sense. Cars generally go down in value as soon as they leave the showroom, so borrowing makes no sense at all. The only good financial reason to borrow to buy a car is either because you will use it to make money (driving it for a job) or save money on an otherwise expensive commute. Other reasons are not good enough. In 7 years, a 10% car loan of FN30,000 will cost FN60,000 to repay, and the car will be almost worthless. Unless you have made that FN60,000 of value by saving taxi fares, train tickets or making Uber commissions, buy a cheaper car or don't buy one at all.

Business Debt

Should you borrow to fund your business? Only if the investment will pay back more than the cost of your loan. It could be something really simple, like the car we mentioned above that you need for work in the "gig-economy," which might be your side-hustle, or it could be something more complicated, like borrowing to fit out a store you want to open. Remember, though, because this isn't a housing loan, it will be higher cost than a mortgage, so you'll need to be really certain that it will make money. This kind of borrowing can of course be very beneficial, but you need to work on your numbers first.

If You Can't Afford It, Don't Buy It

Should you borrow to buy stuff? Should you use a credit card to buy something just because you really want it? Even if you think you "need it," if you can't pay for it outside of your budget, don't do it. Re-evaluate your needs.

Credit card debt is one of the most expensive forms of debt there is. The interest rate they charge will be anywhere from 25% per year to 40% or more. Those two rates double in three and two years respectively. Now think about the thing you want to buy. Would you pay double for it? Because if you borrow on a credit card, the chances are that you will end up paying double!

Let's look at that on a chart.

The top line with dashes shows what happens to a loan with 4% annual interest rate – typical of a mortgage. If we borrow FN100,000, after 10 years we would have to pay back almost FN150,000.

The middle dotted line shows what happens to a loan with 8% annual interest rate, typical of a personal loan. If we borrow FN50,000, after 10 years we would have to pay back over FN100,000 – more than double.

The dark line shows typical credit card debt, with an annual interest rate of 25%. If we borrow just FN20,000 on a credit card, a small fraction of the other loans on the chart, and don't pay it back immediately, the amount we owe will quickly add up to more than if we'd borrowed five times more at a cheaper rate. In just 10 years, FN20,000 in credit card debt will have cost more to repay than a FN100,000 mortgage!

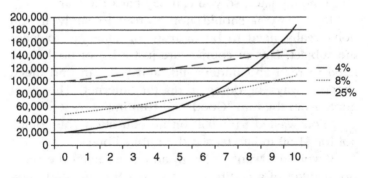

Figure 7.1

Should you borrow to study?

There is no single right answer to this.

For me, the right answer would be that we should all be educated for free, because then everyone in the world would be cleverer and it would be a better place, so obviously I wish people didn't have to borrow to get an education.

That's the way it is in some countries, but not all. In others, students have to pay, and if they don't have the money to start with, they need to borrow to pay for that degree. Should they?

Let's break it down ...

Yes, you should think about borrowing for a course that you can't learn somewhere else for free. If it's "experiential," where you learn by doing, and not from books, then maybe it is worth borrowing because there's just no other choice.

Yes, if you are sure that you will be able to earn so much more after getting the degree (or whatever certificate you get) than you have to pay. A good example of all of those would be studying to become a doctor, which often can't be done for free, can't just be learned about from books or the Internet (whatever we think when we're ill!) and probably will lead you to earn more money later, so you can pay back the loan.

But no, you should not borrow to study if you don't really need to be in front of someone to learn the subject. Lots of courses are just a list of books you need to read and understand, and you can find much cheaper ways of doing it on the internet. The great quote from the film "Good Will Hunting" says it all:

"You wasted $150,000 on an education you coulda got for $1.50 in late fees at the public library."

If you just want to learn, and don't need the security blanket of a certificate on your CV at the end, then save the money and just read. There's an amazing amount of information that's freely available.

You need to work out why you're studying, if it's worth that much money, and if you're really going to benefit enough from the experience, process and qualification that you will be able to repay the debt. Student debt can be cheaper than other types of borrowing, and in some places doesn't always have to be repaid (if you don't earn more than a minimum threshold, for example), but you should assume that you will have to repay it at some point, and that this will reduce your ability to save, delaying your freedom.

All-in-all, whether you should take on debt should be considered on a case-by-case basis. Taking on debt when you are younger can be a smart thing to do, particularly if the debt is cheaper than the returns on the asset, as then the asset will pay for itself.

Remember, though, that you don't own the asset until you've paid off the debt. The Freedom Formula doesn't include debt, only what you own. You aren't free if you still owe money.

"Good Will Hunting" Or The Freedom Formula

How does paying for college compare to the Freedom Formula? To make it easy, let's imagine that the cost of going to college is the same number as in "Good Will Hunting" converted to our Freedom Notes, FN150,000. That includes our rent, food, etc., while we aren't working.

Let's now imagine that our desired annual level of spending is FN50,000, the same as one year of college. So, if we don't go to college, we could already have three years of spending in the bank. Not 25X, but 3X. That's equal to an emergency fund and a combination of investment fund and perhaps a deposit on a house. If we invested that FN150,000 at a rate of 7%, in 30 years it will already be 24X our current spending level (doubling every 10 years from 3 years of spending, to 6, to 12 to 24). We would be very close to our Freedom Formula without saving another penny.

But that's only if we already have the money for our school fees. If we have to borrow, we need to do different calculations.

1. We have to work out how much we will have to pay back.

2. We need to calculate how much we will have to save to do that, just to get back to zero on our Freedom Formula.

If we borrow FN150,000 at a 5% rate, thinking we can pay it off FN10,000 at a time, starting 5 years after we borrow it, we will never pay it off. Never. In 5 years it will have become FN200,000, and then for every FN10,000 we pay off, the 5% interest rate will add another FN10,000 to the total, so we will always owe FN200,000, give or take.

If we double the amount we pay back, to FN20,000, it will take us about 15 years to pay back the debt. To get back to zero. Let's remember, that's where we would have been if we hadn't gone to college. If the FN150,000 was a 3-year course, you would need to pay back 40% of your yearly costs every year for 15 years to get back to where you were before you started.

As a rule of thumb, if college is going to put you ahead of where you would have been without going, you need to be able to save and pay back the equivalent of one year of fees and costs every year: in our example, FN50,000. In that scenario, you would pay off your loans in under 5 years (back to zero) and be able to start building towards your Freedom Formula from then.

Being *Happy Ever After* means being able to earn enough to save your annual college fees every year after you leave.

Paying Off Debt Is The Best Investment

Before we move on to the third kind of ownership, we also need to consider paying down debt.

As we discussed in saving, the first thing you need to do is to build an emergency fund, and then after that you can start investing and decide what assets to invest in. If you have a lot of debt, however, and if it is expensive debt, the best thing you can "invest" in is in paying off your debt.

It may not feel as enjoyable as building up some investments, but the effect on what you "own" will be the same. Remember, "equity equals assets minus liabilities," so it doesn't matter if assets go up or liabilities go down, it will have the same effect on your equity; and it is the equity, the net ownership after debt, that counts.

In fact, paying off the debt may have an even better and bigger impact on your finances than investing. In the early stages of investing, you will probably want to make low-risk investments as you get used to risk-taking. Paying off debt is the lowest risk investment there is, as the return on it is guaranteed, because you have guaranteed to pay that interest rate back to the lender. Yes, unfortunately, it is guaranteed by you!

If it is expensive debt, like a credit card or a personal loan, the rate could be over 20% or even over 30%. It would be nearly impossible to find a low-risk investment that will pay you back that much interest – guaranteed – but paying off those loans will save you those interest payments in future.

You just have to promise yourself to re-invest the savings you have made by paying off the loans, and not take out new loans!

Start An Avalanche With A Snowball!

Paying off debt isn't easy. It's a painful and slow process, and you need all the help doing this that you can get. Not help from people promising to help you on TV commercials or social media advertising – but help from systems and methods that you can use to match your own personality type.

When paying off debt, just like doing anything long and difficult, you need to make sure you feel like you are making progress, and that you are starting to win the battle. If you train to run a marathon, you might not be able to run a couple of miles when you start. The first time you run 5 miles will feel amazing, like a real victory. So will running 8 and ten. Then it will feel great to start running those distances a bit faster, and you can start to see progress in speed and distance. It's the same when you pay off debt.

There are two well-known methods for paying off debt: the snowball and the avalanche. They both start off with the same approach, which is absolutely essential, which is to make your minimum monthly payments on all your debts first (without which, you will incur penalties which will make your debt grow faster), but after that they differ.

1. The "**Debt Avalanche**" is the most rational, sensible and financially logical approach, paying off the highest cost debts first, the ones with the highest interest rates, ignoring how big or small they are. This will save more money over the time you pay down the debts, because those higher interest rates will compound faster, and mean you have to pay back more if you don't pay them off sooner. Leaving the lower interest rate loans until last will mean they won't have increased by as much as the higher interest rate loans would have done. Studies on debt repayment show that people who stick to their loan repayment

plans pay down their debt fastest using a debt avalanche plan.

But ...

2. People aren't always sensible, rational or financially logical, and so sometimes the most effective method is a little less rational and matches our emotions. The "**Debt Snowball**" does just that, and instead of focusing on the interest rate, decides that the first debt to pay down should be the smallest. After minimum payments have been made, all excess repayment funds go to paying off the smallest debt. Once that has been paid off, the second smallest debt gets all the funds ... and so on. The idea is to reinforce the good behaviour with quick wins and happiness about completely paying off a debt.

While studies on debt repayment show that the Debt Avalanche re-payers pay off debt fastest, the same studies show that Debt Snowball re-payers stick to their plan better, because of the encouragement.

So both methods work.

Maybe you know which one would suit you, but why not try both? After all, can't a huge avalanche start with just a small snowball? Arrange your loans in order of size and see if you can pay one off quickly. Don't worry about how much the interest rate is: just see how quickly you can pay off one of your loans (remembering to make all your minimum payments first).

Once you have paid off one debt quickly, see how much you enjoyed that, and then take a look through your remaining debts. See if there are some smaller ones with higher interest rates. Calculate how long it would take you to pay off the most expensive ones. See if you can aim at combining a snowball and avalanche, paying something expensive and quick. If you can't, or it looks too far off, select another smaller debt that you can pay off quickly, for another win. Perhaps by the time you have paid off two debts, you have developed enough of a habit to now tackle one of your bigger more expensive debts, and your snowball really will have created an avalanche.

3. The "**Debt Wipe-Out**" is another option, even though no one talks about it: bankruptcy. Yes, you will need expert advice, and no, it won't wipe out all debts (it doesn't generally work on student loans, for example), but you shouldn't exclude it as a possibility. Rich people do it all the time, so you should consider it too – if you need it.

There are disadvantages, things you won't be able to do in future, etc., but if they aren't things you want to do anyway, and you can't see any other way out of your debt, it makes sense to go bankrupt sooner rather than later so you can clear those debts and start saving.

The Freedom Formula

The third type of Ownership we want to talk about is the best one. It's the answer to the all-important question "How much do we need to own before we never need to work again?"

It's the thing we talked about right at the beginning – the "Freedom Formula". We needed to talk about it at the beginning because it is better to start a long and difficult M.I.S.S.I.O.N. with a good idea of what we are heading towards.

Now we're almost at the end, you should see exactly what the end goal looks like. We've learnt what Money is, how to get Income, why Savings comes before Spending, and how Investing can make our money and our savings work for us. With so many parts of the M.I.S.S.I.O.N. complete, it's important to remind ourselves what that end goal is.

Freedom. Owning our own lives.

So how much do you need to own before you are free? What's your number?

It is so sad that that we don't already know what that number is. Sad to the point of tragic. No single financial number could be more important than the one that tells you how long you need to work for, before you can stop. Before you're free.

We can't know how long we're going to live, when we're going to die, when we're going to meet the person of our dreams, have children with them, win the lottery, or any other such stuff ... but we can work out, really easily, how much money we'll need before we don't need to earn any more. We can know how much we need saved and invested to stop doing what other people tell us to do, when the money we already have will last us forever, setting up the conditions for us to be *Happy Ever After.*

Luckily for us, the equation is really pretty simple: the Freedom Formula is 25 times our annual spending. That's it.

So all we need to do is (1) work out how much we really need to live on in a year and (2) then we multiply that number by 25. Then save and invest until we get that number.

That's it. That's the number you need: 25 times your annual spending.

Happy Ever After Is Forever

One of the regular questions I get when discussing the Freedom Formula is "Doesn't how much you need depend on how old you are?" and it seems like an incredibly sensible question. It's wrong though. It's as wrong as my grandfather.

My grandfather, a drinker and a gambler who was consistently saved from all kinds of trouble by my hard-working, consistently saving grandmother, always insisted that he would never leave any money behind in his will. No one would benefit from his death: and in that, only, he was right. He left nothing behind except for a terrible sense of humour in all his descendants (for which I apologise).

If it hadn't been for my grandmother, he would probably have been living on the street for years.

The Freedom Formula does not work like my grandfather – it doesn't assume my grandmother is going to save it. It works like my grandmother would have done if she had had the right information: the Freedom Formula is designed to leave money behind because it has to.

It has to leave money behind because there is no way of calculating how long we are going to live, and so we can't calculate how much money we are going to spend, and we can't save that amount and not a penny more. It's just not possible.

It might be possible on average, but no one is average, and this time you can't take the risk of being "better" than average, if better means living longer.

If Jack and Jill are 70 years old, and on average, where they live, they can both expect to live until 85, then that's another 15 years of a hopefully full and enjoyable life. They both calculate that they spend FN10,000 a year, so they have both saved FN150,000. They have most of their money in very safe deposits, not earning much interest, and plan to take out FN10,000 a year until there is none left.

If Jack dies after 5 years and Jill dies after 25 years, they were right to expect to live an average of 15 years, but Jill will have 10 years with no money. No money at all. She spent her last FN when she was 85. What does she do for 10 years? Starve? That's not the Freedom Formula.

Let's face it: that story doesn't end well for either of them. Neither of them is exactly *Happy Ever After*.

The Freedom Formula is 25 times your spending because you should be able to withdraw one twenty-fifth (4%) of your assets every year, without it going down in real terms. The money must be invested and generating a return, ideally of 7% or more, and then it should last you the rest of your life – no matter how long you live – and you should never have to worry about money ever again. Yes, that's right, it works forever. We weren't kidding about the *Ever After* part of the title.

An asset base of 25 times your annual spending reasonably well invested means your number should never drop to zero, and you should be protected from the impact of inflation for the rest of your life – even if you live forever.

Is 25X Always The Magic Number?

Twenty-five times is a good number. It's accurate for most people most of the time, but it's in the nature of life that it isn't always that simple, so the Freedom Formula can and does vary a little over time and between countries. That said, in most countries, 4% is generally the highest number which can safely be withdrawn without quickly damaging the value of your portfolio. If you're not sure, it's probably right for you.

Let's imagine a scenario where we have 10 times our annual expenses in assets and savings, and we really want to try to live on that, so we tell ourselves that 10 times is our Freedom Formula. That might be ok if our investment returns were always 10% to 15%, because our investment portfolio would keep going up in value – or at worst stay flat – but 10% to 15% every year is some pretty impressive investing. It's also likely to incorporate some risk.

There are countries and markets where the average rental yield – the amount of rent you get in a year divided by the cost of the property – is 10% or more. If you live in such a place, and you calculate that you can get a yield of more than 10% for a long time, even allowing for the wear and tear of your property, then you may be able to use a Freedom Number of nearer 10 times, possibly using the "three house investment plan" that we will learn about soon.

More normal – and still good – returns, are generally less than 10%. Let's say between 5% and 10%. If that's our level of return, as it will be for most of us if we're lucky, we should only withdraw 4%. If we withdraw 10% in a year, and only make 5%, then our portfolio value will drop to 95% of previous levels.

That's not disastrous in Year 1, but it's not ideal. If the same thing happened again the following year, we would be down at 90%. And so on. It might not sound too bad, and if you're half decent at numbers, you'd know that you could live on the same income for 20 years that way ...

But who lives on the same income for 20 years?

Inflation of around 3.5% will mean that the same income 20 years later will only buy half what it did to start with (remember "The Rule Of 72"), so over 20 years you are effectively getting poorer and poorer. That's not freedom, is it? You may want more money when you're older, perhaps for private healthcare and other such glamorous stuff, not less.

And what if you live 21 years? That's not what we're looking for from our Freedom Number at all. We're looking for freedom and security. Not uncertainty and potential old-age poverty.

Instead, if you live on 4% of your capital every year and make between 5% and 10% returns, your invest-

ment assets will steadily increase, which will help protect you from the effects of inflation too. And then you
will continue to be free.

We might only be able to survive on a 5% withdrawal rate, making our Freedom Number 20X, or we
might want to be safer, and withdraw only 3% a year,
making 33.333333X our Freedom Number, but 4% is
probably the best number to use to start, and so our
Freedom Number is 25X. Once you have saved and
invested 25 times what it costs you to live every year,
then you can consider yourself free.

How Do We Know 25X Works?

For years, I had no idea how much money I needed
to be free, just like everyone else. I just assumed I had
two basic options.

One, I could just keep working for money until I
was so old I couldn't work anymore and then hope I
had enough saved up to last me until I died.

Two, I could hope to make so much money that I
would have an investment portfolio so big that it would
obviously be enough, even though I had no idea what
"obvious" would look like, or how to get there.

Let's be clear here. I had worked in finance for
more than 15 years before I began to work this out. I
had sold billion-dollar deals and was helping to manage hundreds of millions of dollars in investment funds.

So even if this knowledge was only very narrowly
known, I was one of the people who should have
known it; but I didn't, and nor did anyone I knew. I
knew that something like this should be possible, and
was already starting my own theory, using a 3% withdrawal rate, and a 33.333333 ... X Freedom Formula
(a bit more cautious and not nearly as catchy, I'm sure
you'll agree) when I found two other groups using 4%.

Let's start with the oldest and most prestigious: the Rockefeller Foundation. I met with them in their offices in New York, and they told me how their foundation, and most similar big endowments, have a policy of distributing 4% of their funds every year. This amount allows them to keep growing their investment base a little faster than the pace of inflation, which they have been doing for more than 100 years, distributing more than US$17 billion to charitable projects along the way.

That a fund as established, esteemed and, let's face it, old, as the Rockefeller Foundation was using this method made me think that it should work for me. It also made me think that maybe a 3% withdrawal was being a little too cautious. Maybe 25X, to allow a 4% withdrawal rate, could be the Freedom Formula, but it would be nice to hear it somewhere else.

Around the same time, I heard about the "Financially Independent, Retire Early," or FIRE, movement, a group of people who push the boundaries of how early you can be free and independent of working for a living. Prominent among them, not least for his nickname and facial hair, is a character called Mr Money Mustache, whose down-to-earth writing is as far away from the high-falutin' Rockefellers as possible. Despite their difference in approach, Mr Money Mustache used exactly the same number as the Rockefeller Foundation: 4% withdrawal from an asset base that is 25X your spending.

It was the supporting evidence I needed. The Rockefellers showed that the numbers worked in the real world for a long period of time, and the FIRE movement showed that people were putting the ideas into practice today: 25X and the Freedom Formula works.

(I would like to say here that I have huge respect for Mr Money Mustache and the FIRE movement. While most of what I have written here are ideas I have

Maybe John D Rockefeller and Mr Money Mustache
have more in common than they think!

learned during my years of working in finance and investment management, or originated on my own, I often check them against the real world examples of Mr MM and his friends. If Mr MM is saying something similar, I know it's likely to be true and, as he would say, "bad-ass.")

What Should You Own?

Investing is a process. The end result of that process is that you own those investments; so what should you own?

There are really only three key asset types you should think about: interest paying, equities and property. These are likely to make you most of the gains you need to achieve your Financial Freedom.

Keep Interested: If you are risk averse, if you are new to investing or if you are old and retired, assets that pay a fixed rate of interest, like savings accounts, timed deposits and perhaps bonds, are often recommended as the largest part of your portfolio.

As interest rates have dropped over the last 20 years (true at the time of writing), this asset class has become much less appealing and actually dangerous, as they can pay out well below the rate of inflation. For example, if you kept all of your portfolio in this asset class, the Freedom Formula just wouldn't work. You need other, higher returning asset classes.

When older, perhaps a higher percentage of funds can be in this lower-risk asset class, but personally, I would never want much more than a few years' spending (i.e. one year is 4% of portfolio at 25X, so three years would be 12%) in interest-bearing assets, as currently the rates are so low as to be a guaranteed loss-maker. There are other assets that pay more income, with more potential upside, so you shouldn't need deposits for the income stream.

Share It: Stocks, shares and equities are all different names for owning a small stake in companies.

When we deposit money at the bank, we are lending the bank money, so they must pay us back the same amount (and pay us interest). When we buy a share in a company, there are no guarantees, so the returns can be higher or lower than a deposit – or even negative.

With that negative note out of the way, one of the key things to remember with shares is that they not only "share" in the ownership of the company, they also get to "share" in the profits. This sharing is paid out via dividends, a percentage of the net profit the company makes that year, that it doesn't want to re-invest back into growing the company. These dividends are one of the best sources of income you can get from investing, and you can often find good reliable companies paying dividends above 3%, 4% or even 5% – way above what you would get on deposit at a bank these days.

Equities should be the largest component of most investors' portfolios for their combination of growth and income. As an economy grows, good companies at least grow alongside it, if not pushing the pace of that growth faster, and then reward their shareholders for the faith and money they placed in them earlier.

Stocks are likely to be the asset classes that help your portfolio grow to 25X faster than any other, through the combination of profit growth, dividend payment and capital gains. And if nothing else, it's great to own the shares of a company and remember that the CEO now works for you.

Property: Potential And Protection. Let's get something clear right from the very start. We are talking here about property as an asset class, not a pretty place to live. Not a dream home: remember, this isn't a fairy tale, princess!

It is important we stress that right from the start, because that's the way lots of people treat property. They don't think of it rationally at all, they only think of it emotionally, and emotions don't help us invest well.

Sometimes dream homes and pretty places can make great investments, but so too do offices, warehouses, low-cost accommodation apartments, retail outlets, car parks and all other types of property – and you can own these too.

You can buy and rent out the other types of property, often for a yield much higher than the 3% to 5% yield you might get as a dividend on a stock, and you may well make capital gains on this too. Some FIRE-ists base their whole Freedom Formula on this investment structure and do very well at it too.

High-yield rental property is a great small business as you can do it yourself, part-time, and big business doesn't want to compete with you because the size of each investment is too small to make sense for a large company. If you're good at renovation, painting, building or interior design, even better.

Even if you don't want to do that, property needs to be in your portfolio, as it is always likely to be a third of your cost of living, and you should want to protect yourself against that becoming more expensive over time.

Direct/indirect? Passive/active? ETF!

You can invest directly if you want. That means putting your own money in your own savings account, for example, or taking it out and buying property with it. You do both of those things directly because you know how to do them.

If you don't know how to do something, you can hire someone to do it for you, like a fund manager, but traditionally they charged a lot of money (some still do) without seeming to do too much for it. That's indirect.

What do I mean by "do much"? Well, many don't seem very "active," which means investing in things that are very different from the index, or average. You've been able to get index-type performance at cheaper prices for some time, and now with the increasing popularity of ETFs, index-type performance has become much cheaper.

Your overall portfolio will likely be a mix of direct and indirect, passive and active, but be guided in your decision making by whether you know enough to be active and direct, and also by the cost of choosing a manager.

The Three House Investment Plan

Or, as my younger daughter mis-heard it, with very wishful thinking I'm sure, "the tree-house investment plan." Sorry sweetheart, it's 3 houses, not tree houses!

If investing in savings accounts, gold, time deposits, some stocks in the oil industry, banking industry, consumer industries, and also buying a house with a mortgage all seems a little complicated (it shouldn't, don't worry: you will spend a lifetime doing this, not an afternoon), there is a simple investment plan we can create by looking at our own spending that makes sense in places with affordable housing: look away now if you live in London or Sydney!

If we stick to the advice of keeping our housing rental cost at no more than one third of our expenditure, using the other two thirds for all our other needs (savings, food, fun, travel, schooling, healthcare, everything), then we already know that 3 houses will provide all the investment plan we need.

- One house to live in. That's the same as covering our rental costs. We need somewhere to live, and it's in one house. No one needs 2 houses to live in.

- Two other houses to rent out. If these houses are similar to the house you were renting when you were paying one third of your income on rent, these 2 houses will now pay you 2 times that amount, which will equal your non-rent spending.

So you will be back at one third housing, two thirds on other expenses, but now instead of coming from your salary, this is your asset base generating that income: one house to live in, 2 houses to rent out and spend on anything you like.

Looked at simply, if you like the street you live in – and you like the way people around you live – owning 3 houses in that street would be ideal. You live in 1 and rent 2 to other people. The rent they pay you, if it's around one third of their expenditure each, would mean you get to spend on non-rent things about the same amount they do too.

The beauty of this plan is that it benefits if property prices go up, because you still capture the gains from by owning property. And if rents go up, so does your income. Your outcome should be the same as the people around you.

Three Houses? I Thought You Said This Wasn't A Fairy Tale!

I'm aware how it sounds.

You probably can't imagine buying 1 house, let alone 3.

Let's be clear. This is a strategy that will work in some cities, and not in others, and even where it does work it will take time – perhaps a lifetime. Again, this is how you integrate your investing.

I am not suggesting buying three houses in the most expensive cities in the world. If you can afford to do that, please tell me your fairy tale, because I can't.

In expensive property markets, buying 1 house, let alone 3, can often be a bad idea. In cheap property markets it can be a very, very good idea to buy more than 1, and could be the best form of investment. This is how you decide ...

How Many Houses Should You Buy?

Before we decide how many houses to buy, we need to learn a word: yield. That's the amount of rent we get from our property in one year, divided by the cost (or value) of that property.

If the rent on a property is FN1,000 a month, then it is FN12,000 a year.

- If the property costs FN100,000 the yield is 12% (12/100). Nice!

- If the property costs FN200,000 the yield is 6% (12/200).

- If the property costs FN300,000 the yield is 4% (12/300).

- If the property costs FN400,000 the yield is 3% (12/400).

- If the property costs FN600,000 the yield is 2% (12/600).

The amount of rent you can get from property varies a lot. In some places, the amount of annual rental income you receive from your property might be as little as 2% of its value (that's a 2% rental "yield"). In other places and times, the rental yield could be as high as 12%, like the first example.

As a good rule of thumb, it makes sense to buy property when there's a high yield. Using the "Rule of 72", a property with a 10% yield will have paid for itself in just over 7 years, and a 5% yield will pay for itself in a bit over 14 years in yield alone, not worrying about the price of the property going up.

Remembering "opportunity cost" will also help us decide if owning property is a good idea. What return are we expecting from our other investments? If it's high, or the rental yield is low, then maybe owning a property isn't such a good idea. If our return on our other assets is low, then a big difference between rental yield and deposit interest rates will tell us that we'll make more money by buying property.

Let's compare the Freedom Formula with The Three House Investment Plan to see this.

- Jill earns FN20,000 a year, saves 10% of that, spending FN18,000 a year.

  - Her Freedom Number is FN450,000 to make sure that FN18,000 is no more than 4% per year.

- Of that FN18,000 she should then spend no more than FN6,000 as rent and have FN12,000 to live on.

- Jack also earns FN20,000, and he also pays FN6,000 in rent or 30% of his income.

  - Jack calculates the yield of the property he is in. It would cost FN150,000 to buy, so the yield is 4%.

  - If he wants to buy three houses, one to live in and then two that will pay him FN12,000 to live on, it will cost him FN450,000 (FN150,000 for one to live and FN300,000 to get two houses that he can rent out for FN12,000 to live on).

Let's tell a better story.

- Jack does some research and finds out that an area near him has a rental yield of 8%. That means he will only need capital of FN225,000 to buy 3 houses so that he will have 1 to live in and 2 to pay him FN12,000 a year to live on in rental income.

It obviously isn't always like that, though.

- Jill lives in an area with 2% yields and three houses that would pay FN18,000 would cost her FN900,000 (FN18,000 divided by 2%).

- She will probably do better sticking to the Freedom Formula than to try out the Three House Plan.

If you are already renting a house, try doing those numbers for yourself. Calculate how much you are paying as rent per year and then see online how much it would cost to buy something similar near you. If the yield is much higher than 4%, you might be someone who could benefit from the Three House Investment Plan.

Hacking Your Housing?

No, this isn't cutting your house up into tiny bits … although, maybe it is.

In a big sense, house-hacking is doing everything you can to cut back on your housing costs and turning that cut into a property investment.

In short, it involves saving up a deposit on a property that is big enough for you to live in, and for you to rent out some of the space to a tenant. If you can find somewhere, probably something that needs fixing up, where you can rent out a room or two, it's just possible that the rent you get from those rooms will cover the mortgage you have to pay for the whole house.

Your accommodation is now free.

Instead of paying your mortgage, or rent, you can save even faster, perhaps for a deposit on a second property, in which you can rent out every room, because you're still living in the first one … and all of a sudden you've got a property empire.

There are a few more details on house-hacking, plus a link to start your learning process, at the end of this chapter: it's the fastest way to get property into your portfolio.

Back In The Real World: Climbing A Pension Mountain In Your 100-Year Life!

It all used to be so much easier. That's not just a whinge for millennials: it's true. Back in 2002, according to UK insurer Royal London, you could buy an annuity – a guaranteed annual pay-out for the rest of your life – that would pay you 6%. You could buy that and just stop worrying.

Today, you'd be lucky to get an annuity contract that would pay 3.5%. If you chose that route, yes, you'd get some guaranteed money, but the value of it would decline every year with inflation. That's what Royal London calls the pension mountain – the climb to having enough money to cover your retirement.

These returns have dropped in part from interest rates falling, but more is due to longer expected life-spans. As the 2016 book *The 100-year Life* by Lynda Gratton and Andrew Scott explains, "100 is becoming the new 80" in terms of how long we can now expect to live. Every year, human life expectancy goes up a few extra months.

This happy news for us is bad news for companies that offer annuities, and all companies paying pensions. The longer their customers live, the more money they have to pay out, the less money they have left as profit, or perhaps less money to give us as pensions. They also have to charge more to new customers – like you.

Of all the reasons I can think of for you to own the process of being *Happy Ever After,* this is the biggest. While in the past you might have been able to rely on other people to do this for you, not anymore. You are on your own.

You need to own this.

What Woods?

The last picture we drew of the woods, for which we had saved 45% of our income and invested for returns that were 4% above inflation, saw us working and saving into our 40s before we were free.

It's not too scary, is it? We can see our way out of it, at least, and it's a lot better than our first picture where the woods stretched the whole of our lives.

It could be better, though. If we really do "own" this process, make it our own, we could inch our savings rate up even further. If we can save half of our income every month and keep on investing it properly, we could be out of the woods, and free, in just a little over 17 years.

Yes, 17 years.

The difference between not saving and investing any money at all, and saving 50% of your income and investing it for 7% returns, is that you could be out of the woods just 17 years after walking in.

That's so short a walk that you can almost see your way out the moment you step in. It's not so much a forest, it's just a small group of trees. It certainly isn't scary, and it doesn't control your life anymore. You control it.

You own it.

Are You Ready To Own Being *Happy Ever After?*

Ok, who's going to OWN this quiz?

1. **How much of your total net asset base (your portfolio minus any debt) can you spend safely every year?**

   a) All of your returns.

   b) Just the right amount so you have none left when you die.

   c) 4%.

2. **If you can spend the amount you answered in question 1, how many times your annual spending do you need to save to be free?**

   a) Lots.

   b) It depends how long you intend to live.

   c) 25X.

3. **Which is the least risky investment?**

   a) A product that guarantees a 10% return.

   b) The stock of a company you think will make a 10% return.

   c) Paying off a loan that costs you 10% a year.

4. **Why should you plan for your asset base to increase in value every year, even once you stop working?**

   a) To protect yourself from inflation.

   b) Because you don't know how long you will live, and so you don't want the total to go down to zero.

   c) One day, science might really invent the cure for mortality, and we can live forever and ever, so it would be nice not to have to work all that time too!

   d) All of the above, even c, a little.

5. **Who can you rely on to do this for you?**

   a) No one.

   b) Just you.

   c) Both of the above.

6. **If you have a house worth FN500,000 with a mortgage for FN300,000, a portfolio worth of FN400,000, a savings account and emergency fund of FN200,000, what is your financial net worth?**

   a) FN1,200,000.

   b) One MILLION Dollars.

   c) FN800,000.

7. **What's the fastest way to be free?**

   a) Earn more money.

   b) Invest in higher return assets.

   c) Save more, so you decrease your X, the number you need 25 times.

Answers

1. c) 4%.
2. c) 25X.
3. c) Paying off debt is the least risky – because you have to pay!
4. d) All of the above.
5. c) Trust no one. Just yourself.
6. c) You don't own the mortgage. It owns YOU!
7. c) If you save more, you spend less, decreasing the total amount you need to save.

Free Ownership Stuff: *House-hacking*

The biggest thing most people want to own is their own home. The problem for lots of those "most people" is they confuse their own home, with their "dream home" and they assume they have to save for that. Instead, they could get on to the lowest step of the property ladder, and start making their property work for them, to help them up that ladder.

If you want to know more, I suggest going to Chad Carson's website, and in particular this link: https://www.coachcarson.com/house-hacking-guide/ where you will get a really good run down on all the basics of using property as an asset that generates income rather than a liability that costs you money.

"Which makes me wonder why it took a whole book for you to man-splain that to me?"

"Happy Ever After"

The princess woke up lying on her couch by the window. She didn't know when she had dozed off, but it felt as though it had only been a light, fitful sleep as she could remember all of the strange things she had dreamt.

She had dreamt about Jack making lots of money from investing, even though his beanstalk had been a disaster.

About Dick Whittington using his cat as a business to generate something called passive income.

About a wicked witch who had control of the whole wide world, using a web, or a net, or something like that.

About dragons that saved gold coins because they didn't know how long they were going to live.

About how Cinderella wasn't saved by a prince and worked hard to save herself instead. About how princes weren't charming and wouldn't save the day.

And she had dreamed about a frog that talked but didn't want to be kissed – and at just that moment, her pet frog Charlie jumped on to the windowsill, as he always did when she was thinking about him.

She paused, wondering if he would speak. He looked back at her for a long time and then, very thoughtfully, croaked.

"Phew," the princess sighed out loud. "It was all just a dream."

Charlie croaked again, but this time the croak sounded a bit more like a word. "Seriously?" croaked Charlie again.

"What?" asked the princess.

"I leave you to snooze for half an hour and you decide that everything we spoke about is just a dream?"

"Well, it's easier to believe in than a talking frog," she explained.

"Yeah, lots of people find it easier to believe in fairy tales than reality. It's easy to hope that if you don't take responsibility for your own life, someone else will do it for you. It could the king, the government, a handsome prince or your company pension. Or it could even be future-you, who you think will be different from you today, that future-you will start saving and investing later, when you've changed. But it won't happen. Only you, today, now, can change and take responsibility for all of these things."

"Wow!" said the princess.

"Yes," said Charlie. "It's that serious."

"No," said the princess. "Wow, that was a long croak."

When Charlie had stopped being literally hopping mad, he asked the princess what she had learned about life in the real world.

"Life in the real world is muddy," said the princess. "And difficult. And princes don't save you from that. Only you save yourself from it," said the princess.

"And do you remember what you need to be free?"

"I need 25 times my spending to be free, and while I can get that by making more money, I will probably get there faster by increasing my saving and lowering my spending."

"And?" Charlie asked.

"Being happy ever after needs freedom, and to be free, I need to have enough money to choose the best path. I'll need to earn my own money, and not think it's just for spending now, it's there for my future as well. The more I save, the less I will spend and the less I will need to save, because I only need to save 25 times my spending. There will be evil witches along the way who want to make me spend, but there's also magic on my side too, compound investing, which can make my money grow faster. Once it's at 25 times my spending, it should last forever, and then I will always be free to choose my path."

"That's pretty good, princess," Charlie had to admit. "Good summary."

"It is, isn't it?" the princess agreed. "Which makes me wonder why it took a whole book for you to man-splain that to me?"

For the first time in his life, croaks failed Charlie.

"Frog in your throat, Charlie?" asked the princess.

"Erm, I think you'll find it's called frog-splaining," Charlie finally managed to ribbit, "and it's all very well knowing what you have to do, but you also have to start doing it. Given that you already know everything you need to know, now would seem like the best time for **Happy Ever After** *to begin ..."*

The Chapter 8 Cheat Sheet

How We Know When To Start Being *Happy Ever After*

1. Start where you like – earning, saving or investing – but start now.

2. The sooner you start, the sooner compounding will work its magic and set you free.

3. The sooner you start, the more creative you can be with your version of the Freedom Formula. Make your own *Happy Ever After*.

4. Do you think this won't work for you? It will, and it's the only thing that will.

5. In every other stage, we've had seven bullets in the summary, but because we really should start right now, there's no number seven, so you really can …

6. Start now!

CHAPTER 8
N For Now

"Fairy tales are more than true: not because they tell us that dragons exist, but because they tell us that dragons can be beaten."

Neil Gaiman

"Who's Neil Gaiman?" asked the princess.

"He's someone who tells much better stories than me," said Charlie the talking frog. "Although he's not as good looking."

If you want control of your life, there is only one time to start: now.

Not tomorrow, not next week. Not never. It's now.

Nothing ever starts tomorrow. And if you always wait for it, nothing you want to start ever will. Things have to start now – or they never begin.

The sooner you start investing, the more likely you are to be able to take on higher-return investments that should accelerate your wealth, and compound faster into bigger numbers.

The sooner you start saving, putting together an emergency fund, the less likely you are to drop into debt when an emergency arises. The sooner you start earning, the sooner you can start saving.

In fact, if there's a single best reason for starting now, it is that in the future you will earn more, and as you earn more, if you haven't already learnt to save, you will want to spend more. You will become used to spending everything in your salary and it will become harder and harder to scale back. You will start to think that earning and spending are magically linked, that you are doing well living "within your means" not beyond them, that only spending your earnings is a virtue.

It isn't. There's no reason to spend everything now.

The first few years out of school is the perfect time to start saving, because you may never have had any proper income. You might have only ever had money to spend from presents. Any job you get from here, you should focus on saving at least half of the income, if not more.

You are starting with a clean slate of spending, so you can definitely "afford" to save, because you aren't used to your spending. As soon as you get used to spending money, it will become a spending "habit" and as difficult to kick as a coffee, cigarette or drug habit. You will be so used to it that you will think it is impossible to be any other way.

That's why you need to start now.

Even if you're 60 years old, it isn't too late. You can change everything about your future if you start now.

Here Be Dragons – Yes, Right Here, Right Now

This is where you tame your dragons. This is where you rule the world. This is where you conquer what you want to conquer, rescue who you want to rescue and change what you want to change.

The key is that you know how to get to a point where you can have the freedom to choose your battles.

You now know how to create the independence and build the security you need to have in place to fight the fight you really want to fight.

If you follow every stage of your M.I.S.S.I.O.N., when you do meet your dragon, you shouldn't be worrying about whether you can afford the roof over your head, putting food on the table, or paying off credit card debt you acquired distracting yourself by buying trinkets and baubles from whatever shop excelled in distracting shoppers that day.

And you don't have to wait until you have 25 times your annual expenses in investments before you follow your dreams either. What if that dragon threatens the village before then?

I know we said this wasn't a fairy tale, but it wouldn't be a great story either if the hero turned to the village at the climax of the tension, when the day couldn't get any darker, and said, "Erm, I would like to fight the dragon, but I'm afraid I don't have enough savings!"

That's when we would all go looking for a different hero.

A hero who knew how to overcome challenges. Who had done tough things.

You don't need to wait for everything to be perfect before you start your heroics, but you do need to have started doing some of the hard stuff. You can't just rock up with no training and hope to compete. That will only result in failure.

If you get started on your M.I.S.S.I.O.N. early enough, right away, right now, you don't necessarily need to keep saving until you have completed your Freedom Formula.

There's a short-cut. A hack. A secret passage into the back of the dragon's cave, just like there always is for those who are well prepared.

If you start now, and work at it really hard, right away and not give up for at least 7 years, then you can go off and have adventures after that. If you can save half of your income for 7 years, it may be all you need to do to ensure you never need to worry about saving ever again!

Really, that's all. Seven years of saving 50% of your income, and then let the magic of compounding do the rest.

You will need to carry on working the rest of the time, but as long as you're working in a job that pays your expenses, without dipping into your savings at all, those savings will keep on compounding until all on their own, they become your Freedom Factor, and you will be secure for the rest of your life.

Let's use our example of Jill earning FN20,000 again. If she lives on FN10,000 and successfully saves FN10,000, after 7 years she will have FN85,000, if it was invested at 7%.

As we know, this is not enough for her to be free – because we know she will need FN250,000 for that – but that's the thing: all on its own, compounding at 7% per year, FN85,000 will turn into FN250,000 without ever being added to, in just 16 more years.

As long as Jill lives on her own income, not dipping into her investments again, and letting them grow, she will be free after 23 years, but only needs to save 50% for 7 of them.

What will she do for the next 16 years?

- She can live on 100% of her income … in whatever way she likes.

- It may be less money, because taming dragons doesn't pay well.

The Seven-Year Short-Cut

Here's how simple it could be:

1. Work for 7 years and save half your income.

2. Invest it and get a 7% return.

3. Do whatever you want for the next 16 years, just without touching your savings.

4. In year 23, you're free. You'll have 25 times your original spending.

- She may need to spend more money, perhaps on college fees, finding out more about dragon-taming.

- Or travel the world, finding out where the dragons are and what to do about them.

- Or she may choose to have kids, which, as she will soon find out, can be even more expensive than taming dragons, and not entirely dis-similar!

Either way, as long as she saves for 7 years and then doesn't touch it for 16 more, it will become enough money to be free after those 23 years, leaving plenty of time to fight any dragons that may cross her path, or to live happily ever after.

No talking frogs, no magic beans and definitely no dashing princes required.

No More Delays

Remember the last time you thought about starting something. Not the last time you successfully started something, but the last time you thought about trying something, whatever it was …

When you thought about starting a new exercise regime, or giving up a habit that you'd realised wasn't good for you anymore, did you start immediately – or did you wait for a very long time before giving it a go?

Or are you still thinking about starting and not doing it yet?

Welcome to the club!

I didn't start exercising regularly until my mid-30s. I didn't think about what I ate until my early 40s, and then I had to re-start again in my late-40s! I had been drinking too much alcohol for years until I finally decided to do something about it. I thought for years about re-starting my writing before I began opening my laptop every morning.

And I hardly saved a penny until my mid-30s, and even when I started, it wasn't as much as it could have been or should have been.

I would like to claim the reason I didn't save as much as I could is because I didn't know about the Freedom Formula, so I didn't know about the impact it could have on my life. But then I knew all about the benefits of exercising, eating better and drinking less, and those took a long time to start too.

I have to face the fact that I'm a procrastinator.

A hesitator.

A delayer.

If you see that pattern in your own behaviour, then you need to decide to start right now.

Decide which stage of the M.I.S.S.I.O.N. is right for you to begin, where you can get the most impact right now – whether it's earning more money, saving more, spending less or investing better. Once you have identified which of those stages will help you the most, start right away.

- Decide whether you will get a side-gig, what it is, and do it.

- Open a new savings account, so your money can get separated.

- Work out your budget, right now, and see what area you think can be cut back most. Go to www. sevendollarmillionaire.com and see if we're giving away any free sheets from *The Thousand Dollar Journal* and use them!

- Download (and use) a budgeting app and see whether it matches what you think your budget is.

- If you've got savings that aren't earning much of a return, open an account that lets you invest them in other assets right away.

The key two words there are "right away." Take action now, rather than delay a year or two, and you will make immediate progress which could add more than a few years to your freedom.

No More Excuses

You really should start now. The magic of compounding starts immediately and gets stronger the longer you use it, so starting now is always the best time to start.

If you still feel as though something is stopping you, take a good look at what it is and decide whether that thing is more important than your freedom.

- Decide if you prefer freedom or not to disappoint people.

- Decide if it's more important to do the same thing as other people or be free.

- Decide if you like life more than stuff.

If you can answer those questions, you can do this.

You can start now, no matter what you feel about the difficulty or impossibility of achieving real freedom. No matter how small the start is, it's a start.

What other excuses might you be telling yourself you can't start yet? Is it that ...

You're not sure where to begin?

You think you can't save because you have to pay debt?

You think your savings are too small to invest?

You think you've left it too late?

You don't believe that it's possible?

You think you shouldn't start because you won't get all the way to 25X?

You don't want to retire?

You're afraid of doing this?

If you feel you could make any of those excuses, we have answers.

You Don't Have To Begin At The Beginning

If you're not sure where to begin, that's fine. Start where you want. Start where you feel most ready to start.

This isn't school. This isn't dinner with your mother who said you had to eat your vegetables before could eat your dessert. Start with saving rather than earning if you can't earn more or already earn enough. Find ways to cut your spending if that's how you will save more.

Make the change to your life you want to make.

The M.I.S.S.I.O.N. is in a deliberate order because the stages make sense as a journey. If you are to complete the M.I.S.S.I.O.N., you will need to go through all the stages, but if you have already done some on your own, you don't have to go back to the beginning. If you have savings but not enough risk in your portfolio and want to feel comfortable taking more: start there. If you earn well but aren't saving: start there.

This Does Apply To You

It's true that there are people in the world who are too poor to follow the M.I.S.S.I.O.N. I wish there weren't, but that's the reality of the world.

There are also people who can't save because where they live is just too expensive for anyone to be able to save.

You're probably not one of them though.

A lot of the inspiration for *Happy Ever After* came from teaching financial literacy to groups of migrant workers in Singapore, quite possibly the poorest people in one of the world's most expensive cities. They travel there in often dangerous circumstances to escape from the extreme poverty where they live, where there is either no work or unbelievably poor pay. No money to educate their children, perhaps not even enough to feed them.

So they come to Singapore to try to live on as little as possible, so that their tiny salaries, often not much more than a tenth of the country's average income (in perspective, that's equivalent to a USD5,750 a year salary, in the USA), can be saved and sent home.

These migrant workers encapsulate both the types of people to whom the M.I.S.S.I.O.N. shouldn't apply – as they earn very little money and they're in the most expensive city in the world – but they passionately chase their *Happy Ever After*, and they desperately want to achieve it.

Twenty-five times for them might not be a lot of money, but some land to grow crops plus a house (or three), bought and built cheaply in their home village, could deliver their dreams. Earning less than everyone else in the world's most expensive city, they are hungry for tips on how to save, how to invest and how to stop spending. Every time we meet, we discuss personal finance, and they compare their savings habits and listen intently to the ones who managed to save more and spend less.

So even if you are at the very bottom, this can apply to you. You might not feel it applies to you now, and I wouldn't want you to feel forced into doing it, but as soon as you feel you can, as soon as you recognise you can do something about it, then you should, the sooner the better. Now is good.

Debt Isn't The End

Debt is one of the main causes of poverty in the developed world (where, let's face it, no one needs to be poor, nor should they be). You should avoid building up debt whenever possible, and only make exception for the cheap loans used to pay for good assets that will pay you more than they cost, so you can save faster.

If you already have cheap debt that has bought you good, high-returning assets, then well done you. Pay those debts off steadily over time if you choose.

What if you have debt that you didn't buy good assets with? Instead you bought bad assets, or consumer goods, or holidays, or you just ran up a credit card bill. Or you paid for a relative's bills and saved their life. Or you paid your own way through college, and now have a very expensive certificate.

If any of that is the case you probably have expensive debt, without assets that can help you pay them off. You may have no savings at all, plus debt, so you have negative savings. Surely you have a good excuse to say that the M.I.S.S.I.O.N. won't work for you ...

Well, it's an excuse, definitely, and yes, achieving *Happy Ever After* will be harder for you than people without debt, that's true, but not impossible. Actually, it's pretty far from impossible, and not much harder than for people who have no debt.

Let's put it into perspective: from a standing start of zero savings, someone on the M.I.S.S.I.O.N. has to earn, save and invest up to 25X their own annual spending. This is not easy. It can be done, and it can be done in as little as 17 years as we have explained, but it will take some serious commitment.

Debt will make it even harder than that. If your debt is equal to your current annual salary, and to achieve your *Happy Ever After* you intend to save 50% of that salary, then rather than having to save 25 times your spending, you have to save 27 times, because your debt is another two times your spending.

I think you can agree that, while it is harder, the difference between 25 and 27 isn't as big as you might have thought to start with.

That's the way to think about it. However many times your debt is than your current saving or repayment rate, you can add that number to the 25X you need to achieve financial freedom, and there's your new, personalised target. If your debt equals four years of saving, then your new target is 29X.

The good news is how simple that is to calculate.

The bad news is that while achieving 25X can happen much faster because of the magic of compounding, the numbers before 25X, the 1, 2 or however many Xs you have to add to 25X to know your number, will take at least as long to achieve as you think, if not longer. While savings compound by their interest rate, and investments compound by their return, debts also compound – which means you have to pay more money the longer you have them. Pay them fast, and that doesn't happen so badly. Pay them slowly, and this will hurt. So pay them fast. Start now!

The additional good news in your favour, however, is that paying your debt, whether you use the "snowball" or "avalanche" method we talked about before, can get you into the habit of saving that you can carry straight through into saving for your financial independence. There are lots of financially independent people who got there through debt, because of how much they wanted to get out of debt and never have debt again, and so continued on the practice of spending less, saving more and achieving their *Happy Ever After*.

You Have Not Left It Too Late!

One of the key things we need to understand to be *Happy Ever After* is that we don't know when we are going to die. The average life expectancy where you live may be 84, but that means that some people die at 64 and some at 104, and you don't know which one you will be.

That's not as morbid as you might think. If you are 60 today, you could live another 4 years or another 44 … so yes, while you've probably left it too late to take up a career in Olympic gymnastics, you haven't left it too late to become financially independent. You could make a real difference to your last years with a bit of saving done right now. You could do it in as little as 15 years from a standing start.

So no, you haven't left it too late, as long as you're prepared to work hard at saving hard – and start now!

Your Savings Are Not Too Small To Invest

Your first goal with savings is to build an emergency fund. This could save you from disaster, stop you having to borrow from loan-sharks (or similarly expensive credit cards) and become the foundation for your investment fund.

Once you have emergency money set aside, move small amounts of money into your investment fund. Small amounts are actually the best way of investing as then you can take advantage of "dollar-cost averaging" that we learned in "I for Investing," which is one of the best investment tactics in the world. Dollar-cost averaging means you invest the same, small amount of money regularly, which means you automatically buy more investments when they're cheap and fewer when they're expensive.

Small is beautiful – and efficient.

I Don't Want To Retire Either

I have tried very hard not to use the word "retire" in this book, because that isn't what this book is about. I don't want to retire either.

I don't play golf or bingo or bridge.

I don't secretly crave a gin and tonic in the late afternoon.

I don't want to go on a cruise. Ever. Ever. (Again.)

It's the only thing I disagree with the FIRE (Financially Independent Retire Early) movement about. Freedom is so much more important than retirement.

It could be retirement, if that's how you want to be free. It could be working harder than you've ever done before, because you no longer need to work for money and you are free to follow your passion.

That's what this is about, not retirement. It's about freedom. Start now.

Even If You Never Get To 25X, Starting NOW Will Change Your Life

Pretty much the only way you will never get to 25X is if you never save. That's the one guarantee. Spend everything you earn, save nothing, invest nothing, and you'll never be free.

Even saving a small amount will get you there eventually: save 5% of your income a year, invested at a 7% return, you will be at 25X by the age of 87. I know that's not the most appealing argument you've ever heard to save, but that's why you should save more. Save 50% and you'll free after 37, a working life of 17 years not 67.

Can't save 5%?

It can look hard to save 5% at times, particularly when your basic essential spending (rent, utilities, travel) take up a big component of your spend. Here's what you do:

Rigorously, honestly assess if you've never mis-spent in the past. Clothes you don't like. Social spending you didn't need. More expensive choices. Wasted purchases. Attack your possible mis-spending ruthlessly.

Shave 1 to 2% off everything. Negotiate on everything. Don't buy from anywhere that doesn't negotiate. A couple of percent off the rent will get you a long way there.

Find substitutes for everything. Take the train not a taxi. Take a bus not a train. Use a bike, not a bus. Everything has substitutes.

Get to 5% and then never say never again.
But what if you can't keep that up?

If saving at 5% all the time is too hard, never mind. Do it when you can – and do it at least until you have an emergency fund.

There's your "point." Three months of spending tucked in the bank, in some form of investment, is the very best reason to start this now. You may not be free from work, but you have made yourself safe from potential crisis. While free is better than retired, safe and secure is even better than free!

An emergency fund is better than any form of insurance. It's the most important investment. Think of it like the real-world version of an escape pod. Whatever happens to you, you are good for three months. You are safe. You won't need to borrow from someone who will charge you so much interest you can never repay them. Maybe you'll be able to lend to a friend to make sure that doesn't happen to them.

Those all sound worthwhile, and those achievements are a long way short of 25X. They may not equal *Happy Ever After,* but they're a crucial step on the way … and they will definitely make you happier!

Repeat to Yourself: "This Is Possible"

If doing something this different un-nerves or even scares you, you need to talk to yourself more positively. You are as capable of achieving this as anyone else. Don't listen to anyone who says you can't do this, not even yourself. Particularly not yourself. You can do this, and you need to tell yourself that.

"Every day, I am saving my money and investing towards being free."

Say what you like, but say something to yourself that has meaning for you. And say it regularly. Reinforce the idea in your own head that you can do this. And that you will do this. Because you can. And if you believe you can, you will.

Why?

Well, first, and perhaps best of all reasons, it's free. Whether or not you believe affirmations (telling yourself positive thoughts) are cheesy page-fillers from self-improvement hucksters, hocus-pocusery of the lowest order, or jedi mind-tricks that everyone should have in their tool-kit, one thing that is undeniable about them is that they're free.

No one charges you for what you say to yourself in the shower, in the mirror in the morning or on the path where you jog. When you're inside your own head, there can't be an entrance fee. Positive self-talk is always free.

Second, think about any doubts you have about what we've learnt so far.

Do you think you might struggle starting a side-gig or a company of your own? Do you wonder if you really can save that much?

Well ... stop it! Why do you think it's ok to talk to yourself negatively like that, but then think it's bad to tell yourself positive thoughts? Don't let yourself think that self-doubt is honest, but confidence is bad. Shift your thinking about what you can do into the positive. If you can find someone else doing what you want to do, tell yourself you can do it too!

If the first and best thing about positive self-talk is that it's free, the second is that it's a crucial way of building the confidence to fight against any worries and concerns that may get in between you and success.

Tell yourself you can do it, and you have a chance. A much better chance than if you don't. So do it, start telling yourself you will do this.

Third, and kind of scientifically researched, affirmations can become a form of warming up, making your mind and body ready to do the things you want it to do.

If you don't believe me, think about the number of times you have seen sports people go through the motions of their sport before they actually play. We've all seen them, pretending they're doing the thing they're actually about to do. Basketball players take shots with an invisible ball in their hands. Golfers love to take fake swings. All sportspeople, it seems, play an imaginary game.

Part of what they're doing is warming up their muscles to do that thing, but they're also warming up their brains and nervous system to do it too. It's called "priming," this act of getting your brain prepared to do the thing it's about to do, so it can do it better – and more effectively.

Sports people who have to do something like catch and throw a ball have been measured doing this faster than the brain and body are supposed to be able to do it, because they have primed themselves in advance. Every nerve connection, muscle, sinew and thought is activated before the ball is even on the way, knowing exactly what it must do, so no thought process is needed. The body knows what it has to do.

It's one of the reasons why sports people are able to do such amazing things that seem almost impossible.

And not just them. Dancing, acting and all kinds of dazzling skills require a primed brain to be able to achieve them.

It will be the same in your life. If you prime yourself for achievement and freedom, you will be able to achieve things that you might think are otherwise impossible.

You can be *Happy Ever After*. Tell yourself that. Tell yourself that again and again and again, and like a magic spell, it will help it come true.

Start NOW.

The End – Or The Beginning?

"Those sound like magic spells," the princess said to Charlie, her pet talking frog.

"They are probably the closest things that we have to magic spells," Charlie said. *"Just like spells, you have to know the magic is possible, and you have to actually say the spell, over and over again. Once you have done that, it will become stuck in your head, and you will believe you can achieve anything. You can earn more, save more, invest better and become completely free to choose the life you want."*

"No frog-kissing required," agreed the Princess.

"Or prince-kissing either," said Charlie, as though the thought was just as repulsive.

"So, what are you going to start doing first?" he changed the subject.

"Well, I thought I might start a little business to earn some money. I have to do that before I can save, right?"

"Yes, you do, and that's a great place to start. What's your idea?"

"Well I was so inspired by your story about Dick Whittington and his cat, I thought I could do something similar. His cat was only good at catching mice and rats, while I have a pet talking frog that can

*give finance lessons. I could video you doing that
and post it – imagine the hits that would get on–" the
Princess paused.*

*Charlie stared at her, unusually quietly, and some-
thing about the look on his face made her think that
this silence might last for a very, very long time. Some
people say he never spoke again.*

*By then the princess had learned all the lessons she
needed, however, and was able to create her own life,
independently of anyone else, and as a result knew she
would be Happy Ever After.*

The End.

(Or was it just the beginning?)

Can You Be *Happy Ever After* Now?

Unlike Charlie taking a whole book to frog-splain this,
shall we see if we can review everything in just seven
questions?

1. What is money?

    a) It's the part of your life you give up to get it.

    b) It's time and energy and creativity.

    c) It's an efficient way of exchanging and storing value.

    d) It's all of these, so it's something we need to con-
trol before it controls us.

**2. Your money can make more money than you can:
true or false?**

    a) False. Money can't make money.

    b) True. Saved and invested well, your money can
make you more money in your lifetime than you
can earn.

3. Why is the Freedom Formula 25X?

a) Because 25X your spending lets you spend 4% every year, which you can beat with your investing, and so your assets will continue to grow faster than inflation and you never need work again.

b) Why are you looking at b? You've read the whole book already, so you know a is the right answer! There is no possible b or c.

c) See b.

4. Which comes first, saving or spending?

a) In the dictionary, saving comes first.

b) In the M.I.S.S.I.O.N., saving comes first.

c) In life, saving has to come first, because if it doesn't, it won't happen at all.

d) All of the above.

5. How much should you spend on accommodation?

a) If it's really, really, really nice, and you totally love it, then as much as it costs.

b) No more than 30% of your income.

6. Should you own a house?

a) If you're going to live in it for a long time.

b) If you live in an area where property yields (rent divided by house prices) are very high.

c) If yields are high, you could save to buy three houses, and rent two of them to your neighbours.

d) Yes, because renting is giving money away.

e) All except d.

7. Should you take R-RISK when you invest?

a) No, risk is scary.

b) R-RISK is Risk-Return, Integrate, Spread and Knowledge – yes, I'll take some of that.

c) Everything involves risk, even doing nothing, so you have no choice – you have to take risks.

d) b and c.

Answers

1. d)
2. b) Your money can make more money than you.
3. a)
4. d)
5. b)
6. e)
7. d)

The M.I.S.S.I.O.N. Cheat Sheet (Again)

Aim for the **Freedom Formula,** the calculation of how much money you need to be truly free: when you have assets worth 25X what you spend in a year, you need never work for money again. You can work for fun, but you won't need to work for money: earn a 7% return on your investment, spend 4% and the 3% will cover inflation. That's it. You're free to do whatever makes you *Happy Ever After*.

Reaching the **Freedom Formula** requires you to complete a seven-stage M.I.S.S.I.O.N., an acronym for the following:

1. **Money.** Learn what money is, why it is important, when it will be more important, and how to stop thinking about it incorrectly.

2. **Income.** You need to get money into your life, either by working for other people or working for yourself. The more options you have, the better.

3. **Saving.** Save before you spend and you have a chance of being financially free. Separate your money and increase the amount you save whenever you can.

4. **Spending.** Learn to enjoy spending more carefully, negotiating discounts and reducing your careless spending. Cutting back on small things can have a huge impact.

5. **Investing.** The magic of compound interest will grow your savings faster all the time. Don't be afraid to take some risk.

6. **Owning.** Understand borrowing, equity and real ownership, to ensure you can achieve your Freedom Factor and financial independence.

7. **Now.** The earlier you start, the more compound interest will work for you, the less you will have to work. Start now.

Really. Right Now!

It doesn't matter if you are 20 or 50, you can cut your time in the woods down to just 17 years or less, if you start right now.

This could be you …

Thank you for reading, and I really do hope this can help you find your own *Happy Ever After*!

Index